WINNERS

by Simone Bond

Winners

By Simone Bond

Cover Art Created by LeRoy Grayson
Logo Design by Justin Ackerman and Angel Jones
Editor: Anelda Attaway

DEDICATION

This book took 10 years to write, and although it should've been completed a long time ago, it was done in God's timing, not mine. Writing was a passion of mine, and my mother was the only person I shared my thoughts about becoming a writer with, so I dedicated this book to her.

ACKNOWLEDGMENTS

Freda Onelia McKie aka Greta

When it all started, it was only you, I wanted and when it was all over, it was only you, I needed. Mommie, you were everything that I am now. All those years, I tried to find myself and most of what I found I saw in you long ago. Your death was very painful but an awakening. What I learned is that no matter how much you think you can love a person, when death occurs, the love increases tremendously. To the best who has ever done it, my Mommie,

Charles Steven Bond

How could I sum up a great man with a few words? Before this book was ever written, you were there. I would love to thank you for supporting me through every line, chapter, and tear. Along with life's ups and downs, you held on tight and never let me go. Although I was the author, you were my copilot, and I am so grateful to have you in my life. Your love and support during this time gave me one more reason why I love you.

Love you then, now, and forever... Wifey!

Robyn Wilcox

When we first met, we hit it off almost instantly and our love for "Pity Pat" sealed the deal. There's nothing about our friendship I regret but that I took so long to complete this book before you passed. There is not much in life I regret, but that is truly one of the things I do because you were there at the beginning, questioning the characters as I was developing them. Whenever I finally get to Heaven, hopefully, no time soon…save a seat for me at the card table.

Love you, Robyn!

ACKNOWLEDGMENTS

Dakota, aka Chocolate Chip

You are my ray of sunshine that brightens up my world, near or far. As grandma writes this dedication to you, you're about 6 years old. Right now, you may not understand much about this book, but hopefully, one day, you and I can sit back and have a private book club moment. Always remember Grandma loves you for everything you are and one day will be. TOOSTSIE ROLL, TOOSTIE ROLL, TOOSTSIE ROLL, TOOSTSIE ROLL!

TABLE OF CONTENTS

TABLE OF CONTENTS

INTRODUCTION

Kelis Jordan was once a broken, misunderstood, and stunningly beautiful woman! Some say her nasty demeanor diminished much of her beauty! She was what many of us call mixed, better yet, in today's terms, bi-racial. Her mother was African American, and her father was Asian. The combination of the two races does not often unite, but a beautiful baby was created. She was 5'7 and weighed 150 lbs. Most of her stature was her legs. She was half-Black with full lips, brown, and slightly slanted eyes. Her hair was cotton-soft and naturally black like the night, and its texture was as thick as her thighs. Her body was naturally perfect, just a little of this and not too much of that. No plastic surgeries have been done as of yet! When determining her race, she only identified as African American ((Black coffee, no sugar, no cream!) The only time she identified with her Asian roots was when she looked into a mirror.

She was raised in a household that consisted of only women: her grandmother, mother, and two aunts. Kelis's mother suffered a nervous breakdown shortly before she was born. Her father's apparent suicide was too devastating for her mother to process, so her grandmother became her guardian. Her grandmother's name was Alaina. She was the matriarch of her family and the core of her story. She was a beautiful person, but if crossed, her bite was as deadly as a black mamba. Her grandmother ran a gambling spot in the basement of her home, and that is where Kelis was introduced into the world of gambling. When most little girls are outside playing hopscotch, Kelis was often seated in the corner of a crowded, smoky room, witnessing adults partying, drinking, and gambling.

Gambling was a permanent fixture in her home, like a table and chair. Once she got to high school, the observer became the participant. While in school, she orchestrated card games in the bathroom, between classes and during lunch breaks. Once she graduated high school, she began losing thousands of dollars regularly. Her gambling addiction ranged costly, and when she was not out hustling people, mostly(men) she was scheming and manipulating whoever.

While in school, she met a cool girl named Sasha. Sasha was from Connecticut, and her family had lots of money. She and Sasha clashed after hello but later formed a friendship that would have its challenges but would sustain its many trials and tribulations. They became the modern-day Thelma and Louise and, behind closed doors, Lucy & Ethel. They did everything together, from running the streets to hitting the sheets. No, they were not lovers, but did sample the same dicks for laughs!

Kelis was breathtaking, and that kind of beauty can make a little boy go home and empty his piggy bank, and an old man contemplate Viagra. But as she got older, she began to realize that she was no longer the prettiest girl in the room, nor did she give a fuck! Men were not irreplaceable, and she valued none.

When she was not looking, a young man name Bleu entered her life. He erupted feelings in her she did not know existed, and being so determined not to fall in love, she purposely destroyed the relationship. Bleu was added to the long list of love loss, and to deal with the pain, she continued to rely on her drug of choice… gambling!

As the years passed, she became very frustrated with how she was living and contemplated getting professional help. On that very day, instead of getting help, she boarded a plane to Vegas. While in Vegas, she met a rich White Diplomat. His name was Mr. Winston Tisdale. He introduced her to a world she never knew existed and financially bankrolled her gambling addiction. On her many travels to Monto Carlo, Venice, Cairo, etc., she gambles with other forms of diplomats, politicians, and Judges. She was hand-fed her addiction with two spoons, and she wanted for nothing. Suddenly, when things between them soared, she was tossed out with nothing but the clothes on her back. Once she returned to Brooklyn, people, places, and things had changed while the demon within remained the same. To maintain the same luxurious lifestyle, she started robbing Peter to pay Paul and owed Preston, too! She had once lived the ultimate life, but that life came at a price she could no longer afford. That is when she learned that "IN ORDER TO WIN, YOU MUST SOMETIMES HAVE TO LOSE."

CHAPTER 1

GROWING UP

K elis grew up in a primarily decent neighborhood. It was once mostly dominated by whites but by the early 60s, it had become a multicultural neighborhood. She lived in a two-family home on Waverly Street. It was the second grey house to the right. It was not visually the prettiest house on the block, but it was indeed impeccably clean inside.

Long ago, an overhead train ran through Myrtle Avenue, and the screeching sounds of the train's wheels could be heard from many blocks away. Suddenly, the harmony of the enormous steel appeared overhead, and then, in an instant, it serenaded you once again from afar.

Kelis was quite known by everyone throughout the neighborhood, practically because of who her grandmother was! Her grandmother was rumored to be a bad ass; unlike most rumors, that was every bit the truth. She was as ruthless as they came but savored her tender side for her family. Once Kelis's mother was declared mentally unstable, much of her time was spent taking care of her daughters, business, and her rambunctious granddaughter. Many days, Kelis had to be tied to her grandmother's hip, order for her grandmother to be able to complete her daily tasks. Her grandmother was very overprotective, so she was never allowed to go too far. When she got older, her grandmother occasionally would allow her to sit on the stoop in front of the house.

At first, sitting alone on the steps was welcoming, but it quickly became a prison. That is when she started sneaking off the cemented steps out of boredom, but thanks to her grandmother's nosey friend, her whereabouts were always revealed.

Her grandmother's friend's name was Ms. Remsen. She was a human security system that lived next door in a beautiful house. She spent more time in her window than in any part of her home. She was just like the mailman; rain or shine, she remained at her post. She reported everything and observed everyone's comings and goings but never saw her own husband sneaking into another woman's home at night. That goes to show you… people see what they want to see.

After many countless ass whippings, Kelis gave up her search for the unknown and made the best of her surroundings. So determined to break free, she decided, if Mohammad cannot get to the mountain, why not bring the mountain to Mohammad?! By the time she turned 12 years old, her entire anatomy had changed, and her grandmother had built a fortress around her. That meant no communication with boys, loose clothing, and bodyguards. While she sat on the stoop, she started witnessing the various amount of people visiting her grandmother's home by the side door. That was the door that led to the basement where more shit goes down than a toilet. Many on their way out were warned by her grandmother to keep it moving and to not even look in her direction. But Kelis was like a bad accident on the road, too scared to look but couldn't help doing so anyway.

One day a slick-talking mother fucker approached her on her stoop. He was dressed like a peacock, so she assumed he was a pimp. He drenched her with compliments about her beauty, but what he did not know was that Kelis was not the average young girl with low self-esteem in search of a daddy figure. Kelis was warned and witnessed fast talking men like him, so long ago. Just by the way she looked at him, he knew she was not one to play with. So, in attempts to impress her, he had to dig deeper in his bag of tricks. He then handed her a hundred dollars and told her that there was plenty more where that came from. As he walked away, all Kelis could do was laugh because she knew he was about to get played. Weeks later, he approached her again with the same tired ass lines and another 100-dollar bill was offered and taken. Then, about a month later, he came to her on those very same steps and asked her to meet him around the corner. He said he would be sitting in a powder blue Cadillac. He was the replica of the pimps in all those 70's movies, all except Ron O'Neal; he was authentic. "Sure, I would meet you around the corner but before I come, I will need a thousand dollars," Kelis said. "What does a young girl like you need with a thousand dollars?" he asked. Kelis said, "It's none of your business; it's either yes or no." Gazing at her pretty face and thick thighs, he agreed. He returned one hour later and handed her one thousand dollars. The bills were in the 20s and 10s and a few quarters wraps. It seems like this man went home and broke into his piggy bank or collected payment from one of his hoes.

Kelis was sitting on her stoop, minding her business, and along came a pervert. She was going to teach this old dude a lesson. Although she was able to hold her own, there are many young girls out here who cannot deal with such slime. She then told him that she'd need a minute for him to go and wait for her around the corner.

Two hours had passed, and he returned. By then, Kelis was no longer on the steps but spying on him from her bedroom window. She can tell he was pissed by the way he was stomping and cussing. A month had passed, and Kelis was tired of ducking him, so she began sitting on her stoop again.

Then, one day, guess who came out of the side door? Dolomite himself. He aggressively walked up to her and grabbed her by the neck, which sent Kelis into a rage. Their confrontation caused a lot of noise, and her grandmother's ears were like an elephant. Knowing that her granddaughter was in trouble, she came running outside with two shotguns and two big men with two shotguns a piece. Once her grandmother approached the situation, the man knew he was fucking with the wrong girl. Kelis's identity was revealed, and all the old player could do was apologize and pray that he didn't end up in a body bag. Her grandmother demanded both sides of the story, but she knew her granddaughter. Everything Kelis explained was precise, but she lied about him giving her one thousand dollars. She said it was a hundred and only gave that back. There are often many sides to a story, the story told by those involved and the truth. When the dust settled, Kelis was put on punishment, not necessarily because her grandmother didn't believe her side of the story but because of her entanglement with him.

That day, going forward, her grandmother believed she had too much time on her hands, so she was given chores to do daily. Chores that should've been given a long time ago. One day, short of staff, her grandmother ordered her to clean the basement. However, cleaning the club during the day is not a hard task to complete. During those hours, the club has a different vibe; hardly any music is played, just a few stragglers from the night before.

One night, her grandmother was exhausted, and she told Kelis to put down the mop and tally the receipts. In order to tally the receipts, you must also count money, so the money must add up to the receipts. Playing accountant was just part of the thrill, but counting the money became an obsession. The entire environment affected her, and the Pandora box had opened. Working at the club was a punishment in the beginning, but it later became something she looked forward to doing.

Every day after school, Kelis would hurry home and head straight to the basement. At first, her grandmother was overwhelmed by Kelis's enthusiasm for work but later noticed just how much she enjoyed it. Therefore, once six o'clock came, she was ordered to go upstairs and do her homework. Kelis was aware that after that time, the club was a totally different environment and going upstairs was like going back to the cemented stoop.

Laying up in her room, she could hear the soulful sounds of Marvin Gaye, Otis Redding, and Gladys Knight, combined with the joyous sounds of laughter. One night, she was awakened by the same melody and decided to go downstairs to get a cup of warm milk. While in the kitchen, the vibrations of the music intrigued her to follow its rhythm. She would then slowly tiptoe through the beaten oak wood floor that crackled as she walked slowly across them. The uneasiness of the doorknob confirmed that the door was unlocked. The steepness of the stairs made her legs unsteady and she had to rely heavily on the railings.

Once she approached the door, she was greeted by a tiny opening that required a measurable small eye. The uniqueness of the crowd had changed, and the people were dressed much better and sexier. The very dim, smoky room was absorbed with laughter and greasy talk. The crowd was enormous, and they all swayed vigorously simultaneously and aggressively to a slower, sensual beat. It was slow grinding at its best… aka fucking standing up!

As she continued to watch with caution, she was snatched up surprisingly from behind by her grandmother. Once again, she received another ass whipping, and that, too, she took for the team. From then on, her grandmother could do nothing to keep Kelis from peeping in or sneaking in. After multiple ass beatings and punishments, her grandmother realized that it was nothing she could do about her granddaughter's infatuation. Kelis was mistakenly exposed to a life she created, and her only offense was to teach her granddaughter everything she knew about the business. Unfortunately, much of the business wasn't pretty and if her granddaughter was going to be a part of it, she was going to teach her all the bullshit that comes along with it. Surprisingly, Kelis knew more about the business than her grandmother realized. I guess all those years of doing what she does, Kelis paid a lot of attention.

Surely, she was out of control, but out of control, children become out-of-control adults. I believe her grandmother spoiled her rotten because of her mother and father's absence. She too, felt guilty about the many hours she had to spend to make a living for her family. So basically, her grandmother and the streets raised her, and material things were often given when her grandmother felt the guiltiest. Kelis's dependency on beautiful things started the day she was born, and she was given the best of everything, starting from her first sleeper to the current wardrobe she has today. She had a personal stylist, and I am not talking about the celebrity stylist June Ambrose. Her name was Linda Thompson, the best booster to come out of Brooklyn.

Linda was a heroin addict and the sweetest person between fixes. Some days, unexpectedly, Linda would stop by the club, dope sick, in hopes of a sale. Many times, her grandmother would not be there, but Kelis would always buy something from her whether she liked or needed anything. Quiet as it's kept, Linda was Kelis's confidante. Linda thought of Kelis as a little sister and saw a lot of Kelis in her. She always tried to talk to Kelis about the hard knocks of the streets and definitely drugs. Boosting was her profession, but Linda could have been anything she wanted to be. Turns out Linda attended Princeton and got introduced to heroin by her professor. Linda, too, was a beautiful girl and thought life owed her something, and when she was not looking, life handed her a curve ball. Linda was the best in the business. For example, she was able to get minks and designer bags and would occasionally walk out of a few prestigious jewelry stores with diamonds on her fingers and a couple of Rolex watches on her arm. Her grandmother's entire mink collection was thrown out of Macy's window in the back on Livingston Street in the arms of Linda's accomplices. That year, her grandmother bought Linda's entire bundle, and thereafter, minks were worn by the entire family, like people wear sweaters. Linda later died of Aids and was the only person Kelis ever heard of planning their own funeral, down to the flowers on her casket and outfit worn. One day browsing through items in Linda's bag, Kelis saw a beautiful dress, some satin gloves, and a brooch. Thinking those things were for sale, Linda sadly interrupted Kelis and said that those things were going to be worn when she dies. That is as real as anyone has ever been to Kelis and as long as she lived, she will never forget her.

Many years later, when she was dealing with her own addiction, she thought of Linda and often wondered if she had been alive, how disappointed she may have been in her. All those days, Linda talked to Kelis about her addiction; but Kelis never connected the dots until now. What Kelis later learned is that all addictions are real, and until anyone is faced with any, that is when they would fully understand.

Growing up, everything was self-explanatory, and what you did not understand, you better ask somebody. Being raised by a prominently strong Black woman was hard for Kelis. Her grandmother felt that naturally be born her daughters and granddaughters would born with the same strengths. FOR ALL OF THOSE THAT STRUGGLING WITH ANY ADDICTION... HANG IN THERE BECAUSE LIFE ITSELF IS AN ADDICTION, AND WE CRAVE THE DESIRE TO WAKE UP EVERY DAY!

CHAPTER 2

KELIS'S PARENTS

Kelis's mother's name was Mercedes. She was the oldest daughter of Kelis's grandmother. She and Kelis's father met when they were 17 years old in their last year of high school. Mercedes was very athletic and the many trophies on her mother's mantle proved how great she was. Kelis's father's name was Domino Lee Jordan. He was Asian, very smart, and handsome. He was uniquely-tall with golden bronze skin, slanted eyes, and chiseled cheekbones. Domino and Mercedes dated privately because his parents were very prejudiced and her mother was very overprotective. They were two very young people that quickly fell in love and the more their parents forbade their relationship, the more they were destined to be together. Kelis's grandmother was well aware of their relationship, thanks to her friend Ms. Remsen observing everything in her window.

It was earlier reported that her daughter was being walked home daily by this boy and he never departed without a kiss. Her grandmother was not a fan favorite but kept her cool, considering she, too, was once a teenager. Domino's parents' attitude was strictly the opposite, allowing their prejudices to overpower their thoughts and reasoning. Therefore, as time went on, his parents grew furious and forbade him to stay away from Mercedes, but he refused. So, when Mercedes when got pregnant, this made matters worse. His parents took him on what was supposed to be a trip back home to Japan, but he was never allowed to return.

After months of pleading and begging, he fell into a deep depression.

For months, his cries went unheard and eventually, he hung himself from a tree at a luxurious hotel. The devastation of losing their only child prompted them to never return to the United States. No note, phone call, but just a "For Sale" sign on their lawn stating their business A private investigator confirmed the news of her father's death and their whereabouts. Mercedes was never given the luxury to say goodbye and being unable to do so contributed to her breakdown. They were the modern-day Romeo & Juliet, same ending just a different cause of death.

After Domino's death, Mercedes went into a deep depression and isolated herself. Considering she was pregnant, many were concerned but figured once the baby was born, things would change. There is nothing like the birth of a baby to bring joy all around and the best medicine given to a new mother.

Finally, Kelis was born on September 5th, a hot Labor Day. In the beginning, she was a joyful distraction; then suddenly, her cries outweighed her giggles. A continuously crying baby can be a bit nerve-wracking for just about anyone, but to an emotionally unstable mother, it could drive them insane. Kelis's grandmother effectively guarded and observed the situation, but when she started noticing Mercedes's inattentiveness towards her grandchild, something had to be done.

Many nights her grandmother was awakened by her granddaughter's cries and when she went to check on her, she found a dazed-out Mercedes and a baby covered in shit. Dirty diapers and soured bottles were always piling up around, and on many occasions, Mercedes left the baby unattended.

After careful analysis, Mercedes was temporarily put away in a mental institution. Having her committed was the hardest thing her grandmother ever had to do, but she was left with no other options. Mental illness is not always easily detected, and it is a topic many do not want to talk about, mostly because of embarrassment. We all struggle with some form of mental malfunction. Some people know how to recognize the signs and get the proper help, while others tend to avoid it and spend their entire lives struggling to be a better person. It shouldn't have to take someone to throw themselves or someone onto a subway track to finally be diagnosed with mental illness.

With Kelis's mother away, her grandmother's job got harder. She donned many hats and becoming a full-time guardian was not something she signed up for but was something she had to do. Early on, Kelis's grandmother taught her how to accept what had happened to her mother, but Kelis often wonders, when will her mother accept what has happened to her?

HEARTBREAK IS VERY PAINFUL, WHETHER SOMEONE WALKS AWAY OR DIES... A LOSS IS STILL A LOSS! A MIND IS A TERRIBLE THING TO WASTE!

CHAPTER 3

KELIS FAMILY MEMBERS

By now readers, everyone should have a description of Kelis's grandmother. Her name was Alaina, and she was born in South Carolina. She and her husband, Joseph, came to New York when she was 16 and he was barely 18. Long ago, people married early and not necessarily because someone was pregnant, but that was expected. Joseph had a cousin who moved to New Your two years prior he told him about being in Brooklyn for fourteen years and three babies born when Kelis's grandfather was killed. He owned his own car repair shop and was killed in a robbery gone bad.

Her grandmother's middle child's name was Porsche. She was as wild as a caged tiger and would scratch you in an instant. She fed into that middle child syndrome and always felt invisible and unappreciated. Her need to be the center of attention was deadly, and Kelis, being her mother's number one priority, made Porsche feel like she always needed to sharpen her claws. Kelis's grandmother always tried to equally show love to them all, but Porsche seems to have needed more attention than others. The old myth that the squeakiest toy needs the most oil is so true in this case.

From as far as Kelis could remember, they never got along and maybe never will. Once Kelis got older, she learned that her aunt's issues had nothing to do with her and no longer entertained her aunt's behavior until her promiscuous ways interfered with Kelis's life.

Porsche had a liking for young boys and went basically to the playgrounds in search of them. She believed younger men made her look young, not alone a fool. She was also in the business of paying for dick but had an issue sharing it. Kelis believed in neither, and that is where they definitely part ways! Talks of Porsche could go on forever, so, in the meantime, we are going to move on to the most important person in Kelis's life, her aunt Lexus.

She was her grandmother's baby girl, intelligent and compassionate. If not for the DNA, there is no comparison to prove her relations to the family. Lexus looked just like her father's baby sister and had a gentle, quiet personality like her mother. Lexus has always been different and has always stressed her mother out about it. She and Kelis were only seven years apart and Kelis considered her to be more like a sister than her auntie.

Growing up, Kelis wanted to be just like her and followed her around like a sick puppy. Once Kelis got to high school, she was well on her way to creating her own identity but still believed her auntie was still the coolest chick on the planet!

As a child, Lexus stayed to herself and definitely away from the club, while Kelis and Porsche were always front and center. Lexus wanted no part of that life but understood her mother's need to make a living. Finally, she graduated high school and wanted to go away to college, but her mother felt like her wanting to go away to school was really her running away from the family.

Once they all got to a certain age, a lot of things changed, along with their bra sizes! It was time to have that long-awaited conversation, not the birds and bees but who, what, where, and why. Not that she felt she had to, but this was going to be a one-time conversation, and it would not be repeated ever again. She was proud of who she was and by this time in her life, she did not care about those who had a problem with the way she lived her life, even her daughters and grandchild. It was an all-man-on-deck talk, and when it was all over, they all left the scene of the crime with a better knowledge of who (Aliana) was and how she was created! It was straight talk, no chaser! The narrator gave it to them raw but had no choice because she was schooling her babies. She started off by saying that her ability to make bologna taste like steak and a person smile, even when they did not want to, was a gift from God! However, when she started selling dinners, she had yet to learn where it would take her. Her only intentions were to make a few dollars to be able to take care of her family. The gambling thing, just like cooking, was something she always did with friends and family, but when the profits poured in from cutting the games, that kind of money allowed her to give them the things she had never had. So, for every chicken fried, card plucked or dealt, it was worth it. Ms. Alaina was a jack of all trades and mastered the hell out of all of them!

After years of grinding and hustling, her body started showing signs of despair. Long hours wreaked havoc on her body. Many of her aches and pains were attributed to diabetes. The disease robbed her of the ability to run her club the way she once did. Running a club is harder than it looks, and it takes more than setting up tables and pouring liquor into a glass. Managerial skills, determination, and aggression are needed to bake that cake. When she started getting sick, small things were first to be neglected, then came the big things. Deliveries weren't arriving on time, if ever. Receipts were not meticulously organized or calculated precisely, and the books weren't adding up. Kelis's grandmother's business was on the brink of bankruptcy, but before it could get better, shit got worse. Her grandmother was a tough broad and vowed to get a handle on her diabetes and business, but we all know even Superman was taken down by kryptonite.

SOME SAY FAMILY IS EVERYTHING, AND I SAY ONLY IF ALL THOSE ON BOARD BELIEVE IN THAT TOO!

CHAPTER 4

HIGH SCHOOL

Today is September 8th, the first and last year of school for Kelis. She has finally become a Senior and is so excited. On the first day back, many of the students, along with the faculty, look forward to getting acquainted. Many have such high expectations for the new school year, but by Christmas break, the school year cannot be over quick enough. Kelis attended Bay Ridge High, an all-girls school located in Fort Hamilton, Brooklyn. She had other intentions of going to another school, but with mediocre grades and bad reported behavior, Bay Ridge was her only alternative. Although Bay Ridge was not a bad school, it lacked many accolades. Normally, many parents would have a problem with a school that doesn't offer their child an excellent education, but their no-boy policy is what got Kelis's 'grandmother's attention. She believed if Kelis attended an all-girls school, she would be able to focus more on her studies. What her dear grandmother seemed not to realize was that boys were everywhere and that her issue with them was not the same as they had with her.

Once Kelis turned 14, she was stacked like pancakes, and very mature. She never went through a corky stage, accompanied by acne and braces. She went straight from one pimple to perfection. All throughout high school, she never made many friends, mostly because of it. Bay Ridge was not just an all-girls school but a multicultural school. So, since Kelis was half Black and Asian, she finally had an opportunity to interact with other bi-racial kids.

Senior year is so exciting for many students. It's filled with regents' exams, SATs, and preparations for the big dance, the prom. College is not on Kelis's to-do list, but it is something that she would not rule out. Although a college education is designed to give an individual the ability to excel at their highest academic level, it does not often guarantee great success. It has been strongly proven that many uneducated people have successfully succeeded without a college degree. Choosing not to go to college is not highly recommended but if so, your chance of having great success is not doubtful but less unlikely.

One day, Kelis was walking to her homeroom class and accidentally bumped into a girl named Sasha. Neither one of them said sorry, but serious eye contact was made, and they parted ways. Normally, that kind of interaction would get Kelis started, but these days, that was a small thing to a giant. Then, one morning, they crossed paths again when both their rides almost collided in the school's parking lot. Once again, no words were exchanged, but eyes rolling.

Turns out Sasha and Kelis were phantom celebrities at Bay Ridge, both driven daily in fly-ass cars, Kelis in a convertible BMW and Sasha in a Phantom. Each car was fabulous, but to them both, they were cages on wheels. They were both being chauffeured mostly because of their parents' need to control and keep a tab on their whereabouts. It took a lot for these two to become friends, mostly because they recognized the comparison and did not want to accept what they saw. But how did a girl like Sasha, whose family has all the resources and clout, end up at a school like Bay Ridge? It was later revealed that Sasha was expelled from her last school because she went against rules and regulations and got into a relationship with a freshman. A month into the secret affair, she dumped the poor boy, and he was heartbroken. The pain was too much, and he threatened to drop out of school. Since his parents practically founded the school, she was the one expelled. It was not fair, but she had no leg to stand on, considering this was the last of four schools she had been expelled from in six years. That incident was the iceberg that brought down the Titanic. The embarrassment had her family fleeing town, and that is how they ended up in Brooklyn. This time, Sasha was blackballed, and no other prestigious private school was going to entertain her behavior for no amount of money. Brooklyn hosts other schools, but her parents were also overwhelmed with the no-boy policy. However, their friendship is sealed after Sasha helps Kelis from getting her ass jumped in the girls' bathroom.

Everyone knew that Kelis hosted card games in the school's bathroom, so one day, while waiting for students to come to play, two girls walked in. She was alone but not scared, but since it was a 45-minute lunch break with 20 minutes remaining, she decided to leave. Normally, her thirst for the game would've had her waiting up to the last minute. There were plenty of times; 10 minutes was more than enough to bankrupt a mother fucker.

These days, she was determined to graduate, so no more cutting classes, but after school, it's on. As she began to walk down the hall to her next class, she suddenly remembered that she had left her bookbag in one of the bathroom stalls. She swiftly ran to retrieve her belongings, and as she was leaving the bathroom, the two girls who had entered a moment ago came in while she was trying to exit. One of the girls' names was Electra. They both shared the same homeroom and had a hatred for one another, more powerful than most Democrats have for Trump.

Electra's sister's husband was a cop, the worst kind... a crooked cop! He got fired from the police force many years ago and was only able to get jobs securing department stores. Linda Singleton, a famous neighborhood booster, told Kelis that one day, she got busted in Bloomingdale's department store, and he was the arresting officer. Instead of going by the legal jurisdiction, he ushered her into the back of the store and made her perform oral sex on him. However, Linda was not his only victim; many girls got busted in his store and were forced to do the same nasty act. Word on the streets is that Kelis started the rumor and will only admit to finishing it. Obviously, since it was her sister's husband, she had it in for Kelis.

So, while leaving the bathroom, Kelis noticed through her peripheral Electra's sidekick tried to grab her, but her cat-like reflexes allowed her to get out of the way. That's when Electra was able to grab hold of her hair. Hair pulling is the best offense in a girl's fight, and since Kelis had so much of it, she was at a disadvantage. A wig or weave could part ways, but when it is your real hair, separation could be harmful. When it occurred to her that she was about to get jumped, Kelis tried to pull the door open to get out, but Electra's friend was able to get to the door before her and slammed it shut. At this point, Electra had Kelis's hold ponytail wrapped around her hand, and that is when Kelis went into survival mode. The idea of getting her ass whipped by this chick was not going to happen. Then suddenly, her grandmother's whippings came to mind. Long ago she vowed that no other bitch alive would ever hand her down the same ass beatings. Therefore, it was showtime, and that is when she grabbed Electra by the wrist and applied some serious pressure. Strong pressures on the wrist weaken a person's ability to hold tight. Once Electra lost her hold on Kelis's hair, she was able to wipe the floor with that bitch. Still not knowing what her friend was up to, Kelis knew her job there was not done. By then, Electra was on the floor with Kelis's shoe pressed down on her throat. Still wondering how all this was going to end, she heard a loud clap. It was her new best friend, Sasha, standing in the bathroom stall with the look of death in her eyes. So that is why Electra's friend never made a move. Momentarily after she almost suffocated the bitch, she lectured them as if she was their parents. She then eventually allowed them both to leave the bathroom, but not before she told Electra to say hello to her perverted uncle. Also, that the next time he makes another woman suck his dick, he's going to eventually find one in his mouth and if not, his ass.

WARNING:

FIGHTING IS NEVER COOL, BUT UNFORTUNATELY, SOMETIMES YOU MAY BE FORCED TO. JUST MAKE SURE IT IS EITHER SELF-DEFENSE OR HAVING TO PROTECT YOUR CHILD BUT LADIES, UNDER NO CIRCUMSTANCES SHOULD IT EVER BE OVER A MAN!

CHAPTER 5

FOREVER MY BESTIE'S (PLUS ONE)

Friendships like Kelis and Sasha's no longer grow on trees, nor are they made in Japan. They were two women from different worlds that somehow did not allow diversity; economic advantages defined their friendship. They were the Urban dynamic duo, but Sasha was so excited about making them a trio.

Long before she and Kelis became inseparable, she was also paired with a girl named Suki. Suki and Sasha grew up in Connecticut, where trees were perfectly manicured, and the grass was greener than money. Every chance she got, Sasha continuously bragged about this girl and what she described; Kelis was quite intrigued, not to mention a little jealous. Knowing how much this meant to Sasha, Kelis knew she had no choice but to engage in this introduction.

After months of avoiding the inevitable, it was finally judgment day. It was parents' teacher's night, so the school had let out early; instead of heading home, Kelis drove with Sasha to her apartment. Sasha lived in an Upscale condo in Upper Manhattan. This was the first time Kelis had ever visited Sasha's home and the brutal traffic made the trip almost impossible. Although luxuriating in a stretched Limo aligned with buttered soft seating sipping lemonade (spiked), made the journey worthwhile. Also, the driver was fine as hell, but eye candy was all he was because Kelis was not interested in Limo drivers, just those who owned them.

Finally, when they pulled up to this high-rise on 72nd street, there standing at attention, adorned with white gloves and shiny mirrored shoes, was a perfectly polite doorman. As the doorman approached the curb, the tires of the Limo easily kissed the sidewalk. Suddenly, the doors to the Limo opened, and they were escorted to the building as if they were walking down the aisle at their wedding. Once inside, the décor trumped the landscape, and the Egyptian marble flooring made the long walk to the elevator divine. The large glass doors inside the elevators magically closed and, in 0 to 10 seconds, they separated. Just when Kelis could not be more impressed, the doors opened to pure luxury in the sky! The apartment was at least 7,500 square feet, and what set the tone upon entering was the glass piano centered in the middle of its foyer. It had a sunken living room, one master bedroom, two guestrooms, an office, a laundry room, four walk-in closets, and 2 ½ bathrooms. Finally, it had two kitchens, one for daily use and an all-white kitchen, just because.

Kelis and Sasha had been friends for some time and neither of them had been to one another's home. Just by how the condo was designed, Kelis knew it obviously had to be decorated by a professional. Each piece of furniture, painting, rug, or vase was uniquely chosen and well arranged. Kelis was in complete awe and had only seen this kind of setup in the homes of people who live foul. Where she came from, only those who sold drugs or pussy could afford to lace their crib like that!

Nonetheless, her home was nice but lacked fabulosity. Let the truth be told- there is a big difference between Maurice Valency Furnishing and Raymour & Flanagan. Kelis was automatically drawn to the lobby of the building, let alone the apartment interior. Sasha's home gave Kelis the ultimate rush and she vowed to someday live in a similar place, if not better. Still so impressed, Kelis continued to walk around the condo with her eyes and mouth wide open. It almost became frightening how mesmerized she was. Kelis was aware that Sasha was used to such surroundings, but after a hundred compliments given, the nonchalant attitude could have taken the day off.

After she gave herself a private tour of the place, Kelis found herself lost in the massive apartment. Turns out Sasha had a personal chef that would appear without a bell or whistle. His timing was on point because a girl was starving and lost. Just when you think the place had everything; a personal "Chef Boyardee" was hiding in the kitchen. He took their orders as if they were dining in our favorite restaurant. Being a creature of habit, Kelis ordered a simple turkey cheeseburger, while Sasha chose to have grilled lobster stuffed with shrimp, baked potato, chives, and sour cream with a Caesar salad drizzled in cranberry vinaigrette.

Eating out was never her thing since, for years, she had her own personal chef, her grandmother. These days, it's all about "eating to live," not "living to eat." Kelis grew up on the best southern food ever made but in order to keep her body beautifully sculptured, no more fried chicken, baked macaroni, or sweet potato pies! Her body was her calling card and she invested in it heavily. However, today, many women do not necessarily have to worry about getting fat., especially when there are ways to remove fat, they do not want to areas they like.

BOOM, finally, the infamous Suki made his appearance. It was like waiting for Lauryn Hill to enter the stage. As soon as she twirled in, Kelis automatically realized Suki was a guy. Not necessarily knowing how to address the matter, Kelis remained tight-lipped. After the introduction, Suki took off to the next room and made no attempts to get to know Kelis.

Therefore, Kelis continued to roam the apartment unbothered. Suki's gestures were well recognized, and Kelis was going to ignore him like she does other bitches. Jealousy had ruled its ugly head, and this was not her first rodeo. For as long as she could remember, women always got agitated when they were in her perimeter. Why are women so insecure about other women, especially gay men? Whether you are manufactured, male or female, there is no reason for any of us to compete with one another. At the end of the day, every woman has a unique qualification that draws the spider to the web.

Miss Suki's government name was Shawn Bolden. He changed his name privately when he was about 10 years old. He has every intention of legally changing it soon. Suki was cute and could run circles around many girls, but a girl like Kelis came with instructions and a "BEWARE" sign. He was a walking billboard and knew how to make anything look runway ready. He knew how to beat the hell out of a face and make any woman look flawless. Suki was also living at the condo and has been residing there privately since he was 16 years old. The condo apartment was once used for her father's out-of-town business acquaintances. Years later, he and his business partners were caught entertaining prostitutes during many of those business meetings. To build a better relationship with his wife and daughter, he allowed Suki to stay at the condo for one year in hopes of getting a jump start on a better life. One year turned into almost forever, and the rest is history. Once Suki realized that if you cannot beat them, join them, he joined the girls in the opposing room, and the trio bonded the way Sasha intended. Suki was what the duo needed, another bad Bitch that came with her insight on both sides of the tracks.

The most priceless thing he shared was the "Do Not List." That was the list with all the down low brothers in the neighborhood names on it! Suki was straight gay and had issues with men who lied about their sexuality. He had never been with a woman before and never had any desire to do so. Let him tell it; he was born a female, and the only thing that differentia him from any woman is that he was accidentally born with a penis. There you have it, the making of the Treacherous Three and, like earlier mentioned…

FRIENDSHIPS LIKE THEIRS NO LONGER GROW ON TREES OR IN JAPAN!

CHAPTER 6

DEATH OF A LOVED ONE

Kelis's grandmother became a prisoner to her bed and by this point, all her affairs were in order. Although she fought hard to recover, her health was declining drastically. Going back as far as Kelis could remember, her grandmother had always been the enforcer, so to see her defeated was heartbreaking. In the end, she was made comfortable, and to keep her dignity intact, they included her in daily activities concerning her business.

Sometime that year, a second mortgage was taken out on her home so they could pay some unpaid bills. Back taxes were the main concern, and when that was settled, peace of mind was rendered.

Her grandmother was her own health advocate, so when she took ill, she researched her condition thoroughly. She had a good friend named Ms. Remsen, who lived next door. Ms. Remsen was as nosey as they come and was named the neighborhood human security system. When she wasn't on neighborhood watch, she was in her kitchen brewing up some concoctions, which did cure some people with certain ailments in the neighborhood. Her biggest accomplishment came when a man down the block suffered a severe stroke and was told he'd never walk again. Her special brew was mixed with her secret ingredient and 100% proof alcohol. It was so powerful that many women drank it in the early stages of their pregnancy in hopes of aborting their babies.

In the beginning, Kelis's grandmother did not believe in the tea, but when her health started declining rapidly, she figured she had nothing to lose. After about a month, her health started improving, and she was drinking more tea than water. She was never 100% again, but her blood pressure went down, and she regained more strength in her legs. Her grandmother became obsessed with the tea and went on a one-woman crusade in endorsing it. More teas were being bought than alcohol from the club, and for every tea bought, you know her grandma got a small percentage.

Time had passed and Kelis's grandmother was back running her club. Then suddenly nosebleeds accompanied by dizzy spells occurred. Her family became very worried about the reoccurrence of health issues, but her grandmother continuously reassured them daily that she was OK. They never bought that story, but what were they to do? Kelis's grandmother was a con artist and had a way with words, but with all the slick talk she finessed, she could not fool the people who knew her best!

So, one morning at five o'clock, she started her day with prayer and while on her knees, she dropped dead. Her passing was more than just a death. It was the end of life for one and a wake-up call for them all. Kelis's mother's mentality was far too fragile, so they collectively decided not to tell her. Although she had every right to know, it would not have registered. Grief separated the family, and everyone was on their separate path to healing.

During those days, Kelis spent a lot of time with her mother, considering her grandmother was the one who spent most of her time with her. Kelis was ashamed that her timecard was not punched as much, but that was about to change. More time spent with her mother was good for them both and she always felt her grandmother's spirit hovering. Kelis did not claim any religion but believed in a higher power.

Graduation was on the horizon, and she had become profoundly serious about her studies. Going to school all day and helping out at the club four nights per week was hectic. However, keeping the family business afloat was necessary, but graduating was just as important. Many days when things got too much, she often remembers that her grandmother often said that life goes on no matter who dies and to not let her passing be any different! Seems like her aunt Porsche is probably the only one who does not have a problem with moving on with her life. Her mother's body was still warm, and every promise ever made had been broken.

Various strangers were now invading their home during the night, and everyone knew, especially Porsche, that was forbidden. Her grandmother made their home sacred and private and allowed her basement to be the only place where she entertained and ran her business. Kelis and her aunt Lexus continuously complained to Porsche about the situation, but their complaints have gone unheard.

Two weeks have gone by, and no arrangements have been made for her grandmother's homegoing. Lexus has been made the beneficiary of her mother's estate, so that meant nothing could be done without her. The tension between the two sisters had thickened because of the power that was given. Power comes with responsibilities, and it is often given to those who are capable of such tasks. Finally, one day, Lexus roused with the sun and the business at hand was addressed… "Good morning, CEO!" Later that afternoon, a family meeting was held, and they all agreed that it was time to send their" Queen" off beautifully. It turns out Kelis's grandmother had a well-handwritten will that simplified her wishes accurately. In her will, she clearly stated her desire to be cremated and privately memorialized with just her girls in attendance. Cremation is like quickly removing a band-aid… and a whole lot less painful. Her grandmother's decision to have a private ceremony was shocking, considering how public she was in her former life. She provided much explanation about a lot of things, but her reasoning for a private sendoff was that her life has always been an open book; therefore, she chose her final chapter to be private. Not too many people will opt to do such a thing, mostly because a funeral will be considered the last official engagement in honor of that person. Don't you know fewer people will show up to your birthday than your funeral? Also, will travel thousands of miles to bid their goodbyes but will not go around the corner or pick up a phone to say hello! Back at the house, emptiness crowded the room, and the constant drip of water vibrated your ears and began to drive you crazy. If not for Porsche's gentlemen friends, there would not be much movement at the house at all.

It was a cloudy Wednesday morning and we arrived at the crematory quite early. Cremation is a lengthy process because it takes some time for the body to burn down to pure ashes. Since there was no formal funeral, we decided to make the cremation a spiritual ceremony. Long ago, planning a funeral took two weeks, in some cases three, especially if the family had no life insurance and had family members all over the globe. Cremation is less expensive and quick and does not require anyone in attendance. Once Kelis's grandmother's body was placed in the fiery oven, reality set in, and it was official: Queen Aliana was dead! Death is weird, and sometimes, it does not sink in until the burial and many months later. Once you finally realize it, grief takes a nasty turn. There are so many levels of grieving, and everyone grieves differently. The timetable is unmeasurable, and just when you think you are in a good place, an unexpected emotion will bring you to your knees, and you are now brought back to day one! The cremation process took longer than they thought, so they all decided to leave and come back the next day to retrieve her ashes.

On their way home, they stopped at her favorite soul food restaurant on Greene Avenue in Brooklyn! She loved the spot because the food was just as good as hers, plus she had a thing for the owner. Mr. Baker was his name, and he owned the restaurant and was a regular at her club for many years. He had a serious gambling addiction that led him to bankruptcy and many times to the hospital and almost to the morgue. The streets spoke volumes about how Kelis's grandmother saved his ass from eviction and various loan sharks. Her grandmother was very generous, but being a smart businesswoman was her true calling. Keeping his money flowing, kept her money flowing, fair exchange, no robbery! If there was something else going on between them, that too she took to her grave.

Once we were seated, Mr. Baker nervously approached the table along with the waiter. We ordered her favorite meal: fried chicken, collard greens, and potato salad. We were a little skeptical because only she knew how to prepare that meal. Once our orders were taken, he sympathetically gave us his condolences. His grieving appeared more like he had lost a lover more so than a business acquaintance. Once he gathered himself, good stories were told, and many more tears flowed. Our visit to her favorite restaurant was like an unexpected repast, not planned but graciously accepted.

RIP... GRANDMA. THE BEST WHO EVER DID IT!

CHAPTER 7

GRANDMA! CARD GAMES

What comes to your mind when you think about a college sorority. I think about a group of women who take a pledge to organize friendships and support member's goals and admiration. The card world also consists of a large group of women, but the similarities are different. A few friendships are aligned, but many of them are fake. One's aspirations and dreams are occasionally supported but mostly dismissed by haters. The haters are formalized in a group that you may call Click. The women who generate these clicks have no intention of supporting one another or anyone outside of their box. Some of the women are cool, but their Dr. Jekyll, Mr. Hyde personality, comes to light when certain bitches are around. I blame many of their mood swings on the pressures of gambling, but you let many of them tell it, they got it like that. Never underestimate a gambler's ability to lose and never believe a loss is just a loss. Pretending as if you are printing it in your basement is just a front, and when that rent is due, you will really wish you did. To keep it 100, most of us are, one paycheck away from poverty and one scam away from a come-up. Besides gambling, many would not admit that it is also the comradery of others that keeps them coming out. Genuinely, most of them truly love the game, while many of them make a living out of it.

Many believes a hustler and gambler are the same, but they are indeed so different. A HUSTLER goes out to gamble with a game plan. He or she has a bankroll that only extends to what they are willing to lose. No amount of money on the table or in the room drives them to gamble more than they intend to. Their mission is to double or triple their stakes and settle for a dollar more than they had. They are smart and far less greedy than the average player. Nine times out of 10, they always leave as a winner because they know when to fold! A GAMBLER often comes to play with the same intentions, but once seated, something takes over them, and their initial game plan takes another route. They will lose every penny and blame their misfortune on anything from someone standing behind them to being seated in the wrong seat or just the freaking weather. We all know... (it is not the seat but the meat).

Today, millions of people are fighting various addictions, but gambling seems to be the lesser of evils. There is a small mention of its destruction on lottery tickets, cards, and casino walls, but anything the government can capitalize on, they legalize. The product at hand appears less effective when it is profitable. Never have Kelis been on any drugs, but when she got caught up in the world of gambling, her behavior was just as worse than any common strung-out junkie. Her craving to live a fabulous life was just as strong as her gambling addiction and if she had to choose, she was prepared to do so. For many of us that grew up particularly in the hood, playing cards was inevitable. Let's take this shit back to where it originates: once upon a time, our people used to have rent parties. Rent parties were to help the next family during a time of hardship. The community would come together and bring a dish and any amount of money they could spare. It was Black families looking out for one another, something that extinct, like dinosaurs. Those parties were popular, but many families did not reap the rewards because of their pride. Many families privately struggled with their hardship and went hungry or got evicted. Pride is a powerful thing and we as a people make it so hard for any one of us to come to one another, mostly because of feeling embarrassed or being talked about. In results families were put on the street because of that thing called PRIDE!!! It is so sad, that it is easier for a black man to go downtown to the white man instead of going to another black man, his brother!

Card games represent a lot of things and although we all come out to make a quick buck, it is also an unlicensed place to get therapy. Everyone knows plenty of smack is talked while gambling, and in between shuffling, but the best conversations were had on the sidelines. Kelis was introduced into the world of gambling by accident. Her grandmother was preserving her for greatness, and even though she was never allowed to participate in the game, just being surrounded by it captivated her. The smoked-filled rooms and greasy talk, along with the shuffling of cards skyrocketed her adrenaline.

Any gambler would tell you that there's an ultimate rush while gambling. The feeling is no different from alcohol or drugs entering your system. Long ago, people brought their children to these games, but nowadays not too many do. Personally, I think many should leave their children at home, because there is no telling what they may see or hear! Occasionally, someone will bring their teenager or grandchild along to play, but it depends on who is at the table. Many of the players would not gamble with a minor, but Kelis could care less how old they were. She too played many card games when she was very young, but the difference was, these people played at your grandmother's place, and she set the rules.

Remember when dinners were sold for five dollars per plate and drinks were sold for two? The selling of beverages and food no longer exists and is pretty much free at every game. But do not get caught up in the word "free." The word free only applies to slaves and Mandela! Once you have lost about five hundred dollars, you were given nothing for free; and could have fed a small village. Kelis's grandmother was never a fan favorite for selling her dinners or drinks back then. She was always feeding the neighborhood anyway, so her generosity was no different when she had a game. Sharing food is sharing your heart along with opening your home. During the summer, cookouts were where much of the card games took place. From the time the grill got heated until the last hot dog burnt on the grill, cards were still being dealt. All it took was for one person to start shuffling the cards; it was like spraying roaches; one squirt and a million appeared.

Speaking of roaches, a card player is often called one. A roach player is considered someone who plays only their table stakes and hardly ever plays a dime more. I do not call that person a roach; I call that person a smart Mother Fucker! Regardless of what… a roach is a disrespectful thing to describe any human being. A roach carries 33 parasites and pathogens, so the next time anyone thinks of calling someone that nasty bug, they should go home to where most of the roaches are hidden. PS. THERE ARE JUST AS MANY RULES IN GAMBLING AS THERE ARE IN LIFE. BUT SOMEHOW, THOSE WHO FOLLOWS THEIR OWN RULES TEND TO WIN EVERYTIME. IT JUST GOES TO SHOW YOU…THAT IT IS NOT THE SEAT BUT THE MEAT!

CHAPTER 8

PORTRAYAL OF A FRIEND PART I & II

Once Kelis graduated high school, most of her time was dedicated to taking care of her mom and working at the club. College applications were filled out but never mailed because college was a different ballgame and Kelis knew she needed more time to step to the plate.

She was 18, legally grown and feeling herself. Some of the old timers from the club got together and surprised her with a bright red BMW convertible for her graduation. They were literally old fools, because she did not possess a license, but was known to drive without one. Back in the day, many people drove cars without licenses, but times have changed, and those old geezers should have known better. However, the thought was nice but a waste of money because Kelis was chauffeured to school in a limousine daily, thanks to her friend Sasha.

Sasha and Kelis were at the height of their friendship and were dating friends. Not so long ago, for kicks, they would occasionally sample the same dicks. Much of that was because neither of them gave a fuck about the men connected to the package. Going forward, all that nastiness had ended, and the only thing that they may continue to share is maybe a nice bag or some shoes. Kelis also believed that dating friends was corny and taboo, because while in the beginning, everything would be cool, eventually one couple problems become all our problems. Kelis's opinions on the subject went over Sasha's head since these days she is so much in love. Her new man's name was Blaze. She met him at her father's Junior entrepreneur luncheon.

He is the nephew of one of her father's business associates. Blaze was a big-time drug dealer who served some time in prison. Once he got paroled, his uncle pulled some strings and got him into Sasha's father's entrepreneur program. Blaze is a nice-looking brother built for the limelight. He is quiet and very observant, and I'm sure those habits came from being away. He's so dedicated to changing his life around and Sasha seems to be more convinced than his parole officer. Many of his business choices in his past were questioned and that is why he went to jail. However, there are many things about his past he chooses not to talk about, like those underground parties. Those parties were popular in the gay communities and unlike Sasha, Kelis finds him to be very suspicious and, for right now, will be keeping her mouth shut but eyes wide open.

After months of persuasion, Kelis decided to go on a blind date hosted by her friend. She was not fond of blind dates because her date was always satisfied, while she was always left mortified. A good-looking guy doesn't matter unless you are trying to have his baby, but why do they all have to look like Jimmie Walker from "Good Times?" On occasion, there were a few that were not that ugly, but those were the ones that thought buying you dinner meant you were their dessert later. Sasha had this childlike fantasy that one day, she and Kelis would fall in love with friends, preferably brothers. All those years, Kelis had no idea how hopelessly romantic her girlfriend was. What happened to the "love 'em and 'leave 'em" friend she once knew? Her delusional thinking was cute, but she, of all people, knew Kelis was looking for a sponsor, not a husband.

The night had arrived, and the infamous blind date walked in. He and Blaze were friends and met in prison. Oh boy, here we go, Blaze for money laundering and Bleu for murder (self-defense). Bleu was dark as the night, fine with skin smooth as a freshly tarred painted driveway. He had the kind of smile that can make a woman forget her name and unconsciously drop her panties. He was slightly bow-legged because of that heavy meat in between. He was naturally built, home-grown, and fortified with all-natural sweeteners. He, too, demonstrated good manners, but don't let the "yes dear" fool you; Bleu could get gangster in a heartbeat. Months ago, the two of them crossed paths in Vegas and just recently reconnected here in New York.

Sasha and Blaze have just recently started dating and she has become so unrecognizable. So much of her has changed and it has been said a good man can have that effect on a woman. Early in a relationship, a man is often known to be just that, but come spring, they blossom into a totally different flower. Kelis did not believe any man had the capabilities to blossom into anything pure. Where she came from, the first sight of sprouting, they are cut off at the root. Therefore, she was not into gardening and did not interfere with her friend's choice of a man. If so, it could be the quickest way to end their friendship. Her motto was, if you like it, I love it, and if he breaks your heart, I am here!

Her attitude and his arrogance overshadowed their initial introduction. She was indeed not turned on by his cockiness, but everyone knows cockiness is often mistaken for being highly confident. Usually, the nosiest one in the room is the weakest one, but that was not the case for Bleu. Somehow, Kelis aroused something in him that made him unwillingly demonstrate an unlikely behavior. Surprisingly, the more Kelis got to know him, the more subtle, calm, and mysterious he became. Those attributes were once shown and told by family members describing her father and grandfather. Never had any man ever come across to her like that, so their first initial meeting was exuberating and electrifying, but she would never admit it. However, since she was not the kind of girl to get into a serious relationship, immediately once the fireworks started, she dashed it out with cold water. Bleu was and is the perfect man for any woman, but his timing was all wrong. He came into Kelis's life during a time when she believed that all that glittered was not gold and fairy tales were make-believe!

PORTRAYAL OF A FRIEND PART II

Tonight is Suki's 25th birthday party. He has been vacationing in Spain with Leonardo. Leonardo is a beautiful Brazilian Billionaire whom Suki met online. They have been dating for six months, and somehow, he has drawn him into his web. For anyone who knows Suki, every six months, there's a new lover and a wedding invitation that will be going out soon. Sasha and Kelis are hosting this lavish event at Sasha's father's luxurious condominium. Planning an event such as this took lots of planning and coins. Suki is over the top and hard to please and believes in getting his flowers before he dies. The food, theme, and everything in between had to be everything, along with the proper guests in attendance. Money was not an issue since he was such a trustworthy friend to them both. However, Kelis's paper was not as long as Sasha's, but their love was equal. Tonight was more than a birthday celebration. It was a way for them to show Suki how much they loved him, considering this year had been so exceedingly difficult.

Throughout the years, Suki has been struggling with some serious issues and lately has been going to therapy. Many of his deep-rooted emotions stemmed from some unresolved issues involving his parents. Suki left home when he was 16 years old because his parents, mostly his father, did not approve of his sexuality. While on the streets, he befriended some very seedy people and had to do whatever it took to survive. He had become a male prostitute and was hooked on drugs (cocaine). He was introduced to drugs by a former friend, who was also a prostitute. They became very close and looked out for one another on the street. In the beginning, the drug was only used to get Suki through nights of having sex with strange men. The more encounters with strangers, the more drugs were needed. After a while, the drug not only got him through those unpleasant moments but anything else unpleasant life had thrown at him. For some time, his whereabouts were questionable until someone informed Sasha that he was sick in an abandoned hallway in the Bronx.

One cold rainy night, Sasha and her driver went to the location. The building was flooded with addicts, rats, and would-be drug dealers. Sasha being a tough bitch, wasn't afraid of shit. She walked through those broken doors into a barely lit hallway and got her friend out of there. She immediately brought him back to her condo, which was only at the time being used for out-of-town guests. Once her father found out that Suki was living there, he demanded that he leave the premises. Sasha was furious and blackmailed her father. What he did not known was Sasha was aware that the condo was used for business and personally entertaining his female guest. Yes, she was blackmailing her father but also saving a friend. Once Suki moved in, his whole life changed. All he ever wanted was to be someplace where someone loved him for what he was and not what they wanted him to be. Suki has come a long way since those days on the street.

Yes, he is still self-centered and materialistic, but behind all of that, is a frightened little boy.

Timing was everything, and the guest was informed to arrive at 10 o'clock sharp. Putting demands on his guests was ludicrous since Suki was never on time for anything. Ok, Diana Ross, please do not make your friends hurt you. Being the host meant making sure things were done precisely and on time. This party was a two man's job and has somehow become a one-woman's crusade. Somehow, Sasha has gotten preoccupied with her personal life, which left Kelis in search of an assistant. Everything was about Blaze, and since it was not his birthday, she couldn't care less who blew out the candles on his cake.

Finally, the time had arrived, and guests were almost knocking each other over getting into the door. The enthusiasm was justified since this was the party of the year. That old theory that most gay men only associate themselves with beautiful people stands correct. Surprisingly all of Suki's male friends were heterosexual, but many of those bitches, if checked, had a penis. They were all truly replicas of himself, cloned, stuck up and wore way too much makeup.

Furthermore, Sasha knew most of his friends, so she was the overseer of his guest list. Once Sasha became MIA, Kelis had to go to the streets with no leads or phone numbers. Kelis decided that going to the neighborhood hair salon would be her best option. There, on any given day, he could be seen strutting like a peacock. Torturing women made his day, especially the ones that continuously tried to keep up with him but failed miserably every time.

Suki wore the hottest shit and sported the sharpest hairstyles that, on some occasions, made Kelis double check herself. His love-hate relationship with these women was sickening, and I don't know who was the craziest? Spreading the word about his party was like setting a match to a gasoline rag, but just because it was broadcasted, does not mean everyone initially was invited. So, before you come to this party, you better know where you stood with him, or he will ask you to leave on sight.

The party was now at its capacity and everyone who thought they were somebody was present in their best Easter outfits. The drinks were flowing, and many were one drink away from letting the real them be revealed. Suddenly, the door rang and in walked Miss Destiny. She was Suki's friend, from the street. They have always kept in touch but have not seen each other in years. Thanks to Sasha, she informed Destiny about his party, and she dropped everything to be here. But how did she get past the concierge without any of them noticing her, especially in that outfit? He came to represent, and that "sleuths for less" jumpsuit was befitting to his personality. It was a patented leather hot pink low-cut jumpsuit. It was dipped so low in the back; his ass crack was clearly visible according to how the wind blew. He and his outfit were the rave and if it wasn't for everyone waiting for Suki to make his entrance, the night would have been over. Those two were separated at birth and he was definitely someone Suki would love to see tonight.

Once the clock struck midnight, the beautiful people were instructed to move around freely. Free enough to not step on one another's toes but not out of sight. The condo had its own zip code and was filled with beautiful, valuable, exquisite trinkets. There was plenty of Hors d' oeuvre, liquor, and good music. The sound piped through the walls as if they were at a live symphony! Thirty minutes into the party, Sasha and Blaze exited the room and were last seen headed towards her bedroom. After a few drinks, Kelis, too, took a page out of Sasha's book and decided a quickie may be in her near future. As she looked around the room in search of maybe the best dick ever, she noticed Bleu standing at the window observing the Manhattan skyline. Lately, their cat-and-mouse games have become a bit tedious, and it was about time the cat caught his prey. Once she got up close, it appeared that she startled him by the way he jumped. Once he turned around, their eyes and lips met. No words were exchanged, but their bodies spoke an immeasurable language. She gently touched his chest and noticed her clitoris outmatched his heartbeat. At that moment, she knew what time it was, so she placed her hand on his penis, and all was confirmed. In that room, there stood a man with a penis too large not to be in its full erection! Finally, neither of them puts up a fight and allows their desires to lead them where they always wanted to go from the first time, they met…

Once inside the room, she reached for her panties but noticed they had already been removed. In the midst of their passion, she must have dropped them along the way. By the time the door closed, her legs were wrapped around his neck, and all of him was inside of her. Bleu had a nasty, vigorous stroke, and his deep, raspy voice went well with the way he brought it. The tone of his voice reigned high in the streets but was very seductive in the bedroom. Kelis already knew how soft his lips were but had no clue how hard his dick could be. Kelis often demonstrated Alpha tendencies, but Bleu was a strong Alpha male, which gave her no choice but to surrender. She was muffled and lost for words and could only communicate by moans brought on by desire. When it was finally over, the two of them knew something more than sex occurred in that room, but neither at the time was willing to acknowledge it. Suddenly, laughter poured into the room; it was like being spontaneously awakened from a beautiful dream. Kelis then quickly got dressed and joined everyone in the great room. For the rest of the night, she avoided Bleu as if he had Covid-19. She was clearly beaten but still refused to waive that white flag.

As the elevator doors opened, the crowd roared. The red carpet that aligned from the door upon which Suki walked was like the parting of the Red Sea. He twisted and twirled, and Suki, aka Greta Garbo, feet magically never touched the floor the entire night. His eyes widened with delight while tears flowed freely. The night belonged to Suki as he belonged to it. He was a lot of things but often grateful. During his long-rehearsed speech, he graciously thanked all those involved and couldn't wait to announce another wedding proposal. Many wished him well, while many knew this was never going to happen. There in the corner, sprawled out on a 25,000.00-dollar sofa, was Sasha and Blaze. The enormous crowd interfered with their vision of Suki's entrance and from where they were seated, Suki wasn't able to see them as well. Finally, once Suki got up close enough, Blaze was already in the library making a call. Soon after, Sasha joined him. *"Damn, you know a bitch is sprung when a man cannot leave the room to take a business call. But like Kelis earlier mentioned, she would not be getting involved in her friend's business."*

As Suki made his way across the floor, Kelis met him in the middle. The two grabbed one another and it was apparent that they both missed each other. After their emotional embrace, Suki asked where Sasha was. But before Kelis could answer, he went into all of his drama about her not returning any of his calls over the last few months. Suki talking about Sasha is like the pot calling the kettle black… he too, never returns calls. To cut the conversation short, Kelis replied that while he was gallivanting in Brazil, Sasha had fallen in love and did not have much time for anyone or anything. Knowing that they both were creatures of the same habit, all Suki could do was walk away giggling.

The loud sound of trumpets playing was warning the guests that the cake was making its debut. So, all the guests were asked to meet in the middle of the foyer. Just when they all were about to sing "Happy Birthday," Sasha swiftly pushed through the crowd, while holding Blaze's hand. It seemed like the room went dark, and just the three of them were under one huge spotlight. Suki's widened mouth and bewildered brow alarmingly confirmed that he knew Blaze very well. His gestures prompted Sasha to ask if they had met, and before anyone could answer, Suki said yes. Still not connecting the dots, Sasha dismissed the questioning and demanded that they go on with singing Happy Birthday, but Suki refused. Now, everyone in the room's ears were amplified and not a sound was made until an answer was going to be replied. Knowing where all of this was going, Kelis asked the guest to leave the premises, and many were angered by the swift dismissal or because of not getting any cake. Everyone knew Suki's party would be about the drama but never knew that anyone else would out stage him. Like a deer in headlights, Blaze remained quiet and baffled, and that made Sasha slightly suspicious. Once Sasha demanded proper justification, Blaze finally admitted that he did indeed know Suki but couldn't figure out where? The story told was partially true, and somehow, it was enough for Sasha to believe. Knowing that he was lying from the gate, Kelis signaled to Suki from across the room to let it go. She believed that the timing was all wrong, and considering they all were fucked up, the matter could wait.

An hour had gone by, and Kelis accidentally ran into Blaze alone, leaving Sasha's room. He was still drenched in sweat when she grabbed him and pushed him up against a wall. She then got so close up in his face and told him that tonight his ass was spared, but tomorrow was a different day. However, he said nothing, but his eyes said everything. The rest of the night everyone except Sasha was uncomfortable, but Kelis was determined not to let anything spoil Suki's birthday. The night had already taken a bad turn for Suki but as long as he was still the center of attention, he was good.

After a while, the awkwardness became too much but thank goodness the sun came to the party and all the fakeness ended. As everyone was saying goodbye, Suki had left without saying a word. No one addressed the notion, but I am sure his unannounced departure left an impression. Kelis swore on her grandmother that whatever went on with Suki and Blaze would be dealt with, but in the meantime, a bitch needs to sleep!

PS. YOU CAN'T HIDE FROM YOURSELF, NO MATTER WHERE YOU GO, THERE YOU ARE!

CHAPTER 9

BIG WIZ

It has been six months since Kelis's grandmother's death, and since then, many around have also given up on life. Grief is a powerful thing and love of family is the best antidote. During this time, everyone should try to stay together and not allow grief to dominate. These days, business is how they connect, so let's thank God for that. Their home had lost its warmth, and their hearts had gotten colder. Kelis always knew her grandmother was the glue that kept them together, but never did she think her absence would have been this compelling! There was nothing she would do to hear her voice or to smell her fresh collard greens suffocating their home.

Fortunately, the club has been running smoothly and much of its success is because of Kelis's dedication. Her head for business came from observing her grandmother and being a fast learner. When you are taught something, you love, learning is quick and easy. Although she was on top of her game, many would not take her seriously. Was it because she was young, a woman or too fucking beautiful? Many of the old timers and participants were well aware of her age, so why was she legally to fuck but not pour drinks? However, her aunt Porsche's unwillingness to never get old, got old. Their relationship had always had its problems, but it was really her aunt's immaturity that rattled her. Wanting to stay looking young and vibrant is Ok, but Kelis had no patience for a dumb bitch. There is not a woman alive who would not hesitate to stay youthful-looking forever, but that is unrealistically thinking. It is a proven fact that, as you get older, wrinkles and gray hairs will appear, but so should wisdom.

Tomorrow night, the girls are hosting a party for an old-timer named Big Whiz! Back in the day, Big Whiz was a big-time gangster who rolled with the likes of Nicky Barnes, Frank Lucas, and many members of the Harlem Connection! He has always claimed to be legit, but all those close to him knew better and the diamonds and furs he sported did not help his claim. Long ago, pimps and hustlers were uniformed by their attire. They drove expensive cars, mainly (Cadillacs) and wore big fur coats, and every four out of 10 fingers were blinged out with big diamond rings. Nowadays, the biggest drug dealers are low-key and are known to wear dockers and loafers. Big Whiz has always dressed the part and still does. He was a good friend of Kelis's grandfather and later became a business associate of her grandmother. Their friendship conspired after Kelis's grandfather killed Big Whiz's brother. Although it was self-defense, for a minute, Kelis's grandfather was a wanted man. After much speculation, instead of war, a friendship was made.

Big Whiz's brother had made a terrible name for himself out there on the street by cutting many throats. After many attempts to help turn his brother's life around, Big Whiz had no choice but to pray for him from a distance. Big Whiz was a man about business and loyalty and had no tolerance for liars or thieves. Too bad both demonized his brother and made business very bad for himself. That confrontation brought on a lot of heat for her grandfather. He was almost pressured to take his family and leave town. However, her grandparents never ran away from anything but only considered it because of their children. It was her grandfather against a slew of gangsters, and the night Big Whiz's crew came knocking at the door, all her grandfather had was two shotguns, three babies, and a wife huddled in the basement. They were deep in the water of fear but somehow stayed afloat, and nobody drowned. Big Whiz rolled treacherously but he came across an honest man and left his home calm as a lamb. Real men today handle things differently, and every year, to commence the occasion, Big Whiz was celebrated.

After Kelis's grandfather's death, her grandmother continued her husband's obligation. Now, her family is continuing in honor of them both. Lexus feels her parents paid their dues, fair exchange, no robberies. Much of her claim was true, but Lexus was so unaware of the amount of ass-kissing that had to be done in this business. Not only did he not choose to kill their entire family, but he also took on the responsibility to protect them. She was a single woman raising three babies in the land of make-believe. He schooled her about the many crooked cops she may have to pay off and the many cheaters that would come through the door with their personal deck of cards in their pocket and guns in the others! He taught her how to make real money and how to recognize the real mother fuckers from the fake. Many of the old timers that came there that night spent a lot of money, but come tomorrow, they will be snug in their beds by eight. Times were changing, and the club needed a makeover. Kelis's family had the muscle and reputation to do better, but why weren't they? Tonight is Kelis's debut, and it is going to be very interesting, considering many of these guys haven't seen her in a while. The last time Big Whiz laid eyes on Kelis, she was 14 years old, and half of what she has going on. Once her bra size became bigger than her mouth, her grandmother barred her from the club. She had disappeared upstairs like the little girl in "Family Matters," but thank goodness for surveillance cameras, she was able to observe people for many years from her room. From what Kelis could remember, Whiz was a gentle giant that stood 6'5, weighing about 350 lbs. He had a strong jawbone and an enormous nose that overshadowed his many facial abrasions. Many of those scars were a road map that told a horrific story about his life, from his first playground fight to his last prison stint. He was nothing to reckon with, but foolishly, many tried and lived to regret it. He was the Godfather and daddy to many of the children in the neighborhood.

Lately, her aunts have been contemplating selling the house because it has become a liability more so than an asset. Big Whiz has thrown around some numbers because he knows their home is a cash cow. Seems like everyone knows what their home is worth except her aunt Lexus. She could care less what its value and its potential. The thought of selling the house is heartbreaking to Kelis because her grandparents, especially her grandmother, put everything they had into their home. They never outright owned anything; and Kelis is sure they would have never wanted the house to be sold. Those were the dreams of her ancestors and sometimes, those left behind have dreams of their own. Long ago, people partied in the basement of their homes and in run-down shacks called "hole in the walls." Some good times were had in the most not-so-pretty places.

Furthermore, they recently caught up with the mortgage, and in about four more years, hopefully, the house will be fully paid for. However, what difference does that make since everyone wants to move on? Preparation for tonight was in order and the celebration cake was the last thing on the to-do list. Big Whiz was a very superstitious old fool, so every year, he had the same cake down, to the very same hoe! The cake was lemon with vanilla frosting, or was it vanilla frosting on Ms. Lola?

No disrespect, Ms. Lola was one of the prettiest women you could ever lay your eyes on. When crack came into the neighborhood, it destroyed a lot of families and took the soul of a beautiful woman. Many suitors pursued her, even her own husband after he divorced her. He was the joke of the neighborhood, now paying for pussy he once had for free. During those years, is when Kelis learned about same sex relations. Ms. Lola did not discriminate, and if a woman wanted to get down, she got down. She was not the typical crackhead you see roaming through the streets bewildered. With the help of Kelis's grandmother, she ran her operation like a Fortune 500 company. Yea, Kelis's grandmother was a Madame, too, and that explains why, for years, she had seen many scantily dressed women parading in and out of the basement after dark.

When Ms. Lola was out on those streets, she was one filthy crackhead. Kelis's grandmother showed her how to keep herself clean and how to get more than five dollars for a blow job. That goes to show you it is not what you're worth; it is what you can negotiate. She became her grandmother's dearest friend and never did her grandmother introduce her to that lifestyle but showed her how to make it work for her. For most of her life, Kelis patented some of her behavior after Ms. Lola's. She, too, was a beautiful woman with an addiction and used her beauty to get what she wanted. All Kelis's life, she had men eating out of her hands, but these days, those hands are now mostly used for flipping the bird and praying. Fast forward, Ms. Lola got herself together, and every year, an invitation was sent but never replied.

It was now 6:30, and Whiz's goonies had arrived early and dressed like handsome penguins. Many of his friends had passed away, doing time, or were too old to make the trip. For the ones that showed up came impeccably dressed. Oh, how a tuxedo never disappoints and can make any man look good at any age. Most of them were in their late 70s and were glad to be there. Their early arrival was a little unsettling but understandable, considering most of their bedtimes ended when this party was scheduled to start. There was still plenty much to do, and in the condition of these old guys, only a little help was going to be provided. A few of them came in wheelchairs or carried a cane.

As the blue sky vanished, the younger guys from the neighborhood came to pay homage to Big Whiz. Many of them heard about his reputation on the streets or had a father or uncle who knew him personally. Big Whiz was like a national treasure in their neighborhood, and it was very enlightening to see the old gees talk to the young heads about the dos and don'ts of the streets. Many of them had made a lot of money and were very lucky not to have succumbed to that lifestyle. You can tell many were interested in the knowledge, while some paid more attention to the asses in the room. Hustling is like a merry-go-round that, at some point, you must get off. Many become mesmerized by the colorful lights and music and pay no attention to the muffling of sound and flickering of lights. Once the merry-go-round stops, many get off dizzy as a fuck. That is because a well-fed man is forever at a buffet. You have to know when you have eaten enough and have had your share.

For the remainder of the night, Lexus and Kelis were working the crowd, while Porsche was busy sorting through dirty laundry. What a waste of time since many of these guys she had already been with. Finally, Suki and Sasha had arrived, and they couldn't have come at a better time. Sasha was ready to get her hands dirty and Suki his knees. Suki was definitely the life of the party, but tonight, Kelis did not need a hostess but a ranch mule. However, the crowd needed a hype man, and not a door man. The crowd was mostly elderly people that came from a different era, so please Suki don't go near the door. Everyone was cited at their post, but no one wanted to work in the kitchen, but that area needed the most attention.

When it came to Sasha working in the kitchen, everyone got a bit worried since this girl never made her own sandwich or even knew how to turn on a stove. Although she lacked culinary skills, she went into that kitchen and tried to operate two deep fryers and an 800-degree oven. For a minute, she almost pulled it off, but after burning two fingers and nearly her hair from intense flames, she called for her private chef. As much as Kelis needed his assistance, she couldn't help but wonder if he even knew how to fry chicken wings. He once studied at the "Culinary Institute of America," which is the best culinary school in the United States. Much of that education was not needed to fry chicken but more likely "Duck à l'Orange." Surprisingly, he put a spell on those chicken wings and shrimps. He saved the day but come tomorrow, Kelis was going to have to hire an experienced cook and waitress. The task will be challenging because her grandmother was a tough act to follow. Since her death, much of their food served was catered, and many already were complaining about it. Part of why many still came to her establishment was not just for the obvious but for her grandmother's food. By now, the crowd was getting restless, and Kelis & company was doing everything they could do to keep the party alive. It was only so much alcohol, good music, and tits could do. To keep many of them on their toes, they all had to play hostess and work their magic. Even Kelis's aunt Lexus played along. She could not stand anything that had to do with the club and those in it. The one that loved it the most was Suki. He was in his comfort zone, but after tonight, many of them would be questioning their sexuality.

Kelis was a team player, and when she was summoned to the dance floor, she went without hesitation. Kelis was a bad bitch and always wanted to be taken seriously. She knew if she performed innovatively, many would see her in a different light, but she took one for the team anyway. Oh boy, just to watch her walk was a delight, but to see her twerk can stop a man's heart. She wanted to make a name for herself and being seen twerking, especially with a bunch of old geezers, was not the image she wanted.

Suddenly, the guest of honor came bursting through the door with two women on each arm and three bodyguards. He was well-suited in a black tuxedo and red cowboy boots. All night, he got much love and crazy stares. He thought he was looking good, and when you're as old as Big Whiz, you can do and wear whatever you want. His friends were so excited to see him, and throughout the pleasantries, those red boots were obsolete. This was a once-a-year event, and over the years the crowd has gotten smaller but tonight the crowd has reached its proportions. I guess his friends believe that it is best to come celebrate his life rather than his funeral.

By the night's end, everyone was exhausted, and it took the entire crew to make sure everyone was well on their way. There were more access-a-ride vehicles parked alongside the house than a nursing home. Once the last person was loaded onto his or her van, the night was officially over.

CHAPTER 10

LEAVING HOME

Eventually, everyone left the club, chairs were folded, and all receipts were tallied. The rambling of footsteps and giggling was now coming from upstairs. It was apparent that, once again, unwanted guests were upon them! Lexus and Kelis's pleas have gone unheard, and the seriousness of this matter has been duped. What is it going to take to make Porsche understand that bringing unfamiliar men home is unsafe and bad for business? Since rules were set and never followed, Kelis decided her friends were going to stay the night as well. She was tired of following rules that nobody seems to give a fuck about. Two wrongs don't make it right, but it sure does make it even.

Upstairs in her bed was a drunken Suki and a tantrum on the horizon. During this time, when he gets intoxicated, he becomes obsessed with finding a lover or another bottle. He also becomes dramatic, and Angela Bassett is reborn. After kissing the toilet all night by morning, the real Suki returns, once again obsessed with penises and shopping. Since meeting Leonardo, he has made some changes, but they do not coincide with him being in a monogamous relationship. Leonardo is a good dude, but Suki needs someone less naïve and would not hesitate to put his ass in a chokehold if need be. Abuse in a relationship should never be tolerated, but some people need a little toughness projected in their relationships. Just remember, everything that is good to you is not good for you.

Three hours had passed, and Suki had awakened with a headache in search of an aspirin. Kelis had instructed him to go downstairs to the pantry in the kitchen. While in the kitchen, Suki ran into one of Porsche's young playmates holding court. Suddenly, his headache no longer existed, and it was the Suki show in living color. After multiple attempts to get this nigga attention, Suki finally realized the brother was not interested. You would have thought someone had stolen his money or, better yet, his Chanel bag. Sasha seems to always find Suki's behavior hilarious but Kelis wonders how funny he is going to appear to her when she finds out her man use to fuck him. Rejection could be hurtful, but to Suki, it is almost like a death. That fine brother in the kitchen gave Suki a headache Tylenol couldn't cure. He is so infatuated with dick and to think he has one of his own. His fidgety ass got on Kelis's nerves so bad she demanded he left immediately.

It was a very long night, and everyone was exhausted and had retired to their rooms. The sun had made its appearance and Kelis made it clear that it would be no more walking, talking, or stalking! The seriousness of the matter had Suki heading for the door, but only after a long-drawn-out speech. He was such a drama queen, and normally, his antics are entertaining, but not at this hour. One thing about their friendship is they were able to keep shit 100 and no one got offended, only cussed out. Sometimes, their disagreements can get loud and heated but never taken out of content. Lately, Suki has been a bit extra, more than usual, but his behavior is redirected emotion. Since his birthday, the elephant in the room has not been addressed thoroughly. Much of this is not his fault, but the unexpected fork in the road, hopefully, will make Sasha choose the proper lane and not make a U-Turn.

Later that afternoon, after sleeping a mere four hours, Sasha and Kelis headed downstairs to see what was left over from the party. Greeting them at her kitchen table, devouring a very large piece of chocolate cake was Lucky. Lucky was recently hired as part of their security team and is already taking advantage of the perks. He was relaxed with one leg up on the table while his junk hung down to almost the floor. He was fine and the only accessory worn was a large gold chain, a few tattoos, and two deep dimples. Although Kelis never mixed business with pleasure, she did admit that Lucky could have gotten lucky. Her aunt Porsche was still considered a nice piece of ass to most men, but for a young man like Lucky, why was he settling for ground beef when he could get filet mignon. During the interrogation, Kelis reminded him about the dos and don'ts of the job and the rules and regulations of their home. However, Kelis knew Porsche allowed him to cross the lines, but had to warn him to never do it again, if he wanted to keep his job. From the beginning to the end of the conversation, he never got disrespectful and remained attentive to what was being said. Not only was the brother fine, but he also had great manners; you can tell he was raised right. Not that it was any of their business, he told them both that he and Porsche did not fuck as of yet, because she was drunk and fell asleep. Thinking they were alone is why he felt it was safe to walk around naked. "So, you and Porsche never fucked?" Kelis asked. "No, and it seems like maybe never," he said. *"Wow, what a waste,"* Kelis said in her head.

After all was discussed, Sasha and Kelis headed back to her room loaded with treats from the fridge. Somewhere on the steps, Kelis told Sasha to go ahead. Knowing her friend and what she likes, all Sasha could say is, enjoy bitch! Not so long ago, both girls would have fucked him, but today Kelis would be sampling alone. When Kelis returned to the kitchen, Lucky was still sitting at the table. She walked to the refrigerator and got a bottle of water. She then began to drink some and then she poured a little on her hair and what was left in the bottle, she saved for him. She then walked in between his legs and slowly poured the rest on his chest. The entire time, Lucky looked astonished but was ready, willing, and able!

Kelis had on a robe with panties and no bra. As she sat on his lap facing him, he began to suck her left nipple while playing with the other. Suddenly, it occurred to her that not only was the kitchen not comfortable, but they needed to be somewhere she could enjoy him as long as she wanted. Therefore, she returned to her room, and without question, her friend gathered her things and left. Sasha was barely outside the door before Lucky was inside Kelis. In the midst of their entanglement, they got a little too loud and woke up her aunt Porsche. When Porsche knocked on the door, it sounded like the police and just like the police, she came in swinging. Upon entering she quickly grabbed Kelis by the neck and suddenly everything went dark. Once the light returned, Lexus was the one holding the torch.

Somehow, she heard the commotion, from her room, which is almost impossible since she sleeps with earplugs. Sleeping with her ears with ear plugs was something she had been doing since she was a child. Her mother bought her earplugs to drown out the noise coming from the club. So, you know, what she got every year for Christmas.

Fighting was something Kelis always had to do but never did she ever think she would have to fight her aunt. Nevertheless, she felt justified because Porsche has always played dirty, and it was about time she got a little bit of her own medicine.

Lucky was good eye candy and sexy as they came, but Kelis felt entitled to him as her aunt had always felt entitled to her boyfriends in the past. Lexus knew Kelis was just trying to get even, so she was given a pass. She, too, was fed up with the bullshit and used this situation to warn Porsche once again about the no men in the house rule. Other than family, no one was permitted, mostly because of security purposes.

By the time the commotion came to a halt, Lucky had already gotten dressed and left. He eased out the side door like he stole something, but that was OK; his job here was done well. He saved himself from the embarrassment of being thrown the fuck out. The caliber of the three women in the room: Kelis, satisfied; Porsche, never satisfied; and Lexus, mortified! Lexus had no concern over Sasha's and Keli's bullshit and her only concern was making her sister understand the importance of having unwanted guests in their house. It was no secret that they were doing shit illegally, but how they were doing it was nobody's business. Still dazed, from previous events Porsche sarcastically tried to convince Lexus that there were no reasons for concern. Lexus immediately made it clear that under any circumstances, there would be no more pajama parties. One thing for sure, two things for certain: Porsche did not fuck with Lexus. Lexus was the baby, but she would devalue Porsche in a heartbeat. So, after Lexus made it clear where she stood, Porsche quickly apologized. Soon after they all headed back to their rooms. As they all walked up the stairs, Porsche asked Kelis, "Hey, niece, was it good?" Kelis replied, "Hell yeah, and maybe the best fuck I have ever had!"

CHAPTER 11

AUNT LEXUS DEPARTURE

Ever since Kelis's last confrontation with Porsche, she has been spending a lot of time at the condo with Sasha. As much as she and Lexus have spoken to Porsche about the rules of the place, she still does what she wants. Kelis was aware of her responsibility and that meant working long extra hours and every other weekend. She missed being at the house, but in order to keep the peace, she eliminated herself from the situation. Although staying at the condo was fabulous, it was not home. Being with friends and spending some nights together was cool, but to live together was something entirely different. Kelis was born an only child and never had to share her space or candy with anyone. However, a 7,500 sq ft apartment should be big enough for three people, but somehow, it started to feel as if she was living in a closet. Plus, her mother's mental health was declining drastically, and the facility was not that far away.

Once upon a time, it was her family's obligation to take care of her mother, but somehow, it has become a one-woman job. These days, everyone has become preoccupied with their own lives, and Kelis had made her mother her number 1 priority. Her mother's recent setback has her thinking more about her future. Thoughts of going to college were once considered, but she knew in order to get a degree, she would have to be dedicated to her studies. Also, money was needed now and becoming a doctor, or a lawyer, was going to take too many years to achieve. Therefore, getting money now was her main objective. The club's proceeds were very profitable but after the bills and the help was paid, there wasn't much to divide amongst the three. On a daily basis, they were cutting games, selling liquor, and also secretly doing other underhanded shit on the down low. They were pulling in close to 20 to 30 thousand dollars weekly and still Kelis felt they were not making enough. Lexus and Porsche were comfortable with what they were getting, and Kelis could be just as happy, but she couldn't see the profits because she was gambling hers. It's a wonder why her aunts would want to sell the house, since they were comfortable with their current financial income. Many prospects have been considered, to buy the house and nobody has ever asked Kelis her opinion. It's crazy; she is not the reason this place was founded, but she's the only reason it still exists.

Their eagerness to sell so quickly was premature and Kelis started to wonder what their urgency was. Kelis understood money was needed in their quest to move on, but why were they so quick to sell to the first buyer that walks through their door. Porsche would rather sell the house to anyone except her, while Lexus would walk away and not take a dime. However, Lexus did need the money because she wanted to go to school to be a gynecologist, so it would take a whole lot of coins. What a great career choice, considering she has a sister that will need someone to help her care for her litter box. The thought of Lexus leaving saddens Kelis terribly. Although she is moving on to conquer her dreams, it almost feels like a death. Her aunt understood her pain but insisted if she stayed, the lifestyle would hinder her ambitions. Medical school was challenging enough, and keeping the hours it took to run their club would have been almost impossible. Lexus, as we all know, was a different breed; she was never cut out for this life. Unlike Kelis, she was born at a "Pity Pat" table and loved it. Money was not really the issue, but that all depended on what most people call money. Lexus did well by her share since she had no vices. However, Kelis and Sasha were spending it as fast as they were making it.

Kelis was aware that it was time to make better choices for her future. She even once considered selling drugs but, she was done with drug dealer boyfriends and anything else about that life. Once she took inventory of her life, it was quite frightening. She discovered that all she had going on was a pretty face, a fat ass, and a high school diploma. Today, those things could be required by cosmetic surgery and bought online. The silver spoon she once ate from has begun to tarnish and the kingdom where she was crowned princess she no longer rules.

There's a high-stakes poker game going down tonight on the Lower East Side. It was being held at what looked like an abandoned warehouse, but inside it was everything. The owner purposely wanted to create a crumbling exterior to distract wondering eyes that lurked abroad. It's owned by an ex-cop who used to work security privately for her grandmother. He resigned from the police force long ago and is currently up to his old tricks that forced him to resign. Every crooked cop, street punk, and Nino Brown impersonator will be in attendance. Tonight, Kelis will not be rolling solo because going to the Lower East Side at night could be dangerous. All her life she has been highly protected, but these days relies on no other but her real ride or die…9mm.

The sun was beginning to set, and Kelis was luxuriating at the condo, anticipating the evening ahead. The ringing of her phone interrupted her peace. It was the nurse from her mother's facility urging her to come immediately. She had informed Kelis that her mother was having a bad day, and her presence was needed. Without hesitation, she headed out the door, jumped into her car and turned a two-hour commute into a casual walk in the park. As soon as she reached the parking lot, she was able to hear her mother screaming. Immediately, Kelis hurried past the front desk and ran up the stairs. Once she approached her mother's room, she was balled up in a fetal position, screaming profusely! Quickly upon arrival, Kelis wrapped her arms around her but unsuccessfully could not get her to calm down. Normally, when Kelis comes to the aid of her mother, she usually gets a positive reaction. Never had she ever witnessed her mother in such distress. Yes, there have been temper tantrums, followed by loud cries, but never to this multitude. "How long was she like this?" Kelis asked. The nurse replied that she was very temperamental for most of the day, but her mood escalated during the last hour. She also reminded Kelis that many calls were made to her phone but were sent to voicemail. Quickly, Kelis checked her phone and realized there were many missed calls, but she couldn't understand why.

After some time, Kelis was able to calm her mother down. Every so often, her mother has these emotionally erratic breakdowns that are usually accompanied by her being tranquilized. Sedatives are highly recommended, but the side effects are a roll of the dice. Sometimes, a gentle touch and soothing words can be more powerful than any medication administered. It was rough for a minute, but when it was all over, her mother nestled asleep like a newborn baby. The facility uniquely understands the needs of its patients and they go way beyond the criteria for them and their loved ones. Everything is not always black or white; sometimes, gray areas appear. Also, considering what the family was paying, not much else could be asked for.

After a long, quiet nap, her mother eventually awakened peacefully. For most of Kelis's life, she and her mother barely interacted with one another because of her mental illness. Much of their relationship was accompanied by doctors and her grandmother's submission. Once her mother had awakened, she started muttering like usual, but then miraculously, her voice appeared angelic and strong. As Kelis stood in complete awe, her mother started talking about things Kelis knew nothing about or remembered. Then she started talking about being in love, saying that it can be beautiful, but beware of those who do not reciprocate the feeling. At this moment, Kelis wondered if she would say anything about her mother, but when Kelis mentioned her name, she replied with tears. She finally spoke of Kelis's father, saying how angry she still was about him taking his life. In some ways, Kelis identified with her mother's anguish because she, too, had not forgiven her father either.

Her father's death was boomeranged; one woman stopped living and the other was in search of how to. If only her mother could have understood his pain, and that it was what lured him to the choices he made. Part of her healing should have been trying to forgive, and since she did not, she was not able to get better. Being forever bitter is like stage four cancer. If not cut out immediately, it will fester and eventually eat you alive. Seems like much of her mother's memory has gotten away from her, and she seems to only remember the things she should have forgotten. Just when Kelis thought she had spoken her last truth, she reminded Kelis about her courage. She told her that she carries the strength of her grandmother and not only was she born strong, but also beautiful. In the remembrance of her beauty, her mother told her that beauty was skin deep, and it should never be used for evil. Also, she was to never apologize for who she was or settle for anything less than she deserves. As quickly as the conversation started, it ended, and her mother was back asleep, but not before she told her that she loved her! Saying, "I love you," was a rarity from her mother, but it was something Kelis needed to hear.

In the occurrence of today's event, the poker game tonight will have to wait. She was feigning to play cards and her inner gut wouldn't rest. Kelis was a gambler in need of a fix, but she was trying to put her mother first. While her mother slept peacefully, her phone alerted her about tonight's itinerary. That was nothing but the devil making his rounds and thoughts of leaving and coming back came to mind. Just when she thought the devil had won, her mother grabbed her arm as she was slowing leaving her bedside. Looks like the devil had not won, something they both had in common. She took that as a sign and turned her phone off completely and remained still alongside her mother. An occasional catnap during the day is fine, but anything passed an hour is for babies, sick people, and lazy mother fuckers! The facility does a good job of keeping her mother's room clean, but Kelis was never satisfied with their technique of cleaning, since she grew up in a home cleaner than the "White House. So, with a little time on her hands, she" decided to clean her mother's closet. While salvaging through her things, she noticed a small aluminum box on the floor in the corner. In the box were old pictures of her mother and her siblings growing up as children. The pictures were very old, but Kelis was able to make out who and what. Turns out she and her mother shared the same drop lip as a child. Although Kelis looked exactly like her father, she was happy to see that she and her mother had some similar features. As she dug deeper in the box, wrapped in a silk pink handkerchief, was a picture of her father. The picture was dated a month prior to his death. Over the years, Kelis only witnessed one very warp picture of him; so, this was like seeing him for the first time. Therefore, it was like looking in a mirror because their features were so duplicated. His lips were thicker and more masculine. They both shared the exact copper-tone complexion as if the sun betrayed them. The photograph sent chills down her spine while her heart fluttered. Finally, she could see where she came from and thanked him for supplying the ingredients that were needed to bake such a beautiful cake. No longer was she going to not acknowledge her Asian roots because not acknowledging them is not acknowledging her father. Her unwillingness had a lot to do with her grandparents disowning her and their biased attitude is what led him to take his life. The box contained a lot of things treasurable to her mother, along with her diary, his high school ring, and a few old love letters written by him. Browsing through old pictures was one thing, but she was not about to read love letters written from one lover to the next. Those letters will never be shared and will forever be private, and when her mother finally passes, those letters will be buried alongside her. Right between the letters was a nicely folded envelope. She was a little reluctant to open it, thinking it may be more love letters, but she knew the importance of the envelope by how it was neatly managed. Her curiosity (nosey ass) had her by the throat, so she ripped it open. Would you believe it was the original deed to her grandmother's house? All her children's names were listed in alphabetical order, so that meant her mother had every profitable right as her two aunts. All this time, there was much talk about selling the house and nobody ever considered her mother or her only child. This document meant more than part ownership; it meant her grandmother considered all of her daughter's and it didn't exclude her oldest child because of her incapability. That being said, Kelis, being her mother's overseer, meant her mother's business was her business.

TIMING IS EVERYTHING AND JUST LIKE A TRUE GAMBLER, YOU NEVER SHOW YOUR HAND TOO SOON. ALSO, HER MOTHER WAS IN HER FINAL STAGES AND SHE WAS NOT GOING TO WASTE ANY ENERGY ON ANYTHING OTHER THAN HER BEING. P.S IT WAS THE CALM BEFORE THE STORM AND KELIS VOWED THAT THE MINUTE HER MOTHER CLOSES HER EYES, ALL BETS WERE OFF THE TABLE.

CHAPTER 12

BLAZE'S DOUBLE LIFE REVEALED

Suki had been homeless since the tender age of 16. Although he has a very beautiful home to live in, he still considers himself homeless. Leaving his parents' home so young left him hungry for family. Since then, he has cut off all ties with his people, except his cousin Alexandria. She and Suki were very close growing up, and she was the only one he was able to confide in about his sexuality. Many years later, during their separation, Alexandria got hooked on drugs. While on the streets, Suki, too, experimented with drugs but was able to not let it destroy him. Drugs are a powerful supplement and many who innocently experiment with it usually become addicted. After many years of abusing drugs, Alexandria vanished. She was known to disappear from time to time, but after nearly two years had gone by, many had believed she was dead. Turns out, Alexandria had secretly gone to rehab. She entered a program called "We are ready when you are." While in recovery, she met a handsome man named Malcolm. Malcolm was a recovering heroin addict and was clean for only one year. When Alexandria entered the coed program, she was angry, and rebellious, and repeatedly threatened to walk out. One thing about treatment: unless you are under a court ruling, treatment is never forced! Her path to soberness was rough, but somehow, she hung in there and got the well-deserved treatment she needed.

After months of intensive therapy, Alexandria adapted well to living a sober lifestyle. However, her attraction to Malcolm was just as intense as the drugs, she once used. Alexandria came from a very dysfunctional environment. Alexandria witnessed her mother's oldest sister have an open affair with her father. Infidelity is a painful experience for any woman, but to be betrayed by a family member makes it more difficult to digest.

Alexandria's father was a notorious womanizer. He abused women in every way possible and because he was rich, he was excused. Alexandria's grandmother obviously also came from a toxic household because she entertained his behavior. She allowed a man to use her two daughters and that type of shit is sometimes handed down from generation to generations. As Alexandria grew up, she was forced to respect him, but never did he ever respect her or any woman. She later confirmed that the abuse she suffered on the streets was not nearly as bad as what she went through growing up. Malcolm was nothing like any man she had ever known. He was soft-spoken, attentive and literally swept her off her feet. Engaging in relationships in the program was prohibited because they needed their patients to concentrate more on their recovery, than the feelings of each other. After much effort on both parts, they decided to put their treatment first but vowed to continue one day what they had begun. Another year had passed, and Malcolm had completed his stint in rehab. After he left the program, he and Alexandria stayed in contact with one another through letters and phone calls. Then, finally, the day came. Alexandria was done with rehab and on her way to leaving a drug-free, enriching life. Upon her release, they got together as they planned.

Getting to know one another outside of the facility was challenging, but the real challenge was learning to trust one another. Two people with an addiction sometimes do not necessarily make a good fit. You would think that with so much in common, things will automatically gel, but sometimes, too much in common makes things too apprehensive. After a rightful amount of time dating and building the trust that was most needed, they eventually got married. They were well on their way to a fresh start and considering what they had both been through, everyone involved was over the moon. Two years into their marriage, they decided they wanted to have children. After much lovemaking and countless tests, it turns out that Malcolm's sperm cells were damaged from years of heroin use. The couple was devastated and consulted the best doctors, but after much discussion, adoption became an option!

One day, Suki arrived at Alexandria's house during one of his occasional wellness checks. After her last disappearance, they vowed to always check on one another. Alexandria was now living in Long Island, so this was not a hop, skip or jump for Suki. The afternoon was filled with much laughter and fueled by many cocktails for Suki and apple juice for Alexandria. Suddenly, the conversation shifted and got profoundly serious! Alexandria confided in Suki about her and Malcolm's struggles with conception. All options were being considered, but she was considering in vitro fertilization because she wanted to be able to carry her own child. The procedure was pricey and not always on the first try; sperm fertilizes an egg. It could take multiple attempts, costing thousands of dollars each time. Alexandria and Malcolm's finances were not where they should be for a couple who opted for such a procedure. Adoption was the next, best thing and such a beautiful thing to do. Malcolm's inability to have children left him more open-minded and wanting to do whatever it took to make her a baby and happy. Suki was unknowledgeable about the topic but jokingly said he was willing to donate as much sperm as needed. Alexandria laughed at first but then realized that since Suki was a good-looking guy and family, it may not be a bad idea. Thank goodness they were cousins through marriage, or this procedure could have produced a child with a leg for a nose. Alcohol has a way of making a person tell the truth or make promises they cannot keep. When the subject came up again, Suki then again asked to donate his sperm, and this time, Alexandria kindly accepted. To put all her fears to rest, he assured her that he would give up all parental rights and that if she ever needed anything, he would be there, but to not ask him to babysit. He was definitely ok with his decision, since he knew the children would be taken care of by the most loveliness person he had ever known. Everything on the topic was reviewed and all there was left to do was tell Malcolm about the good news and for Suki to masturbate in a cup.

The evening was nearly over when Suki got a frantic, unexpected call from Kelis. She was uptown having drinks with a very good male friend. His name was Diamond. Diamond is a male escort, better yet, a well-paid whore. He was always an attractive man, stemming all the way back to middle school. Every little girl wanted him to carry their books, and it cost them their milk money. Once he got to high school, he elevated his game and charged girls just to walk alongside him. Senior year, he took eight girls to their prom, two in one night, and went solo to his own. How in the hell did he pull that off, it is still a mystery to many?

By the time he was 19, he was done with girls his age and started fucking older women; some were mothers of the daughters he once dated. Older women paid well, but he got bored and moved on to stripping. Stripping put him in a better financial position to provide for himself, but after time, it became degrading and too competitive. Walking away from the pole was difficult but much harder for others. He had started fucking the owner's wife, and when he decided to move on, she nearly died. She then gave him an offer he couldn't refuse. He no longer had to sling his pipe for strangers four nights a week. He was now her personal paid lover, slinging privately for just two. He was given a huge raise and was kept on their payroll. She took care of him for years and even left him a little something in her will. Diamond was nobody's fool; and going forward he professionally took his skills to another level. For now, on, he was preparing for his future and knew that in time he would be getting old. Never would anyone walk away from him without a financial commitment or because the sausage is not as meatier than it once was. Therefore, he was the one to teach Kelis about her worth and having the best two teachers in the world, how could a girl go wrong but somehow did? There are so many reasons why Kelis looked up to this man but right now we must move on.

Diamond was dining at a club called the "Sugar Bar." It was a small, quaint, dimly lit club in Harlem. It was owned by another old bitch he used to fuck. He and the woman no longer get it in, but he regularly frequents the spot because the food & drinks are excellent. While sipping the best Cognac there is, in walks Blaze with a woman on his arm. What was more shocking, the chick was transgender. How did Kelis know the woman with Blaze was a Trans? Considering the dim lighting, those big hands and feet can be seen anywhere. Diamond was in the dark about Kelis's emotions, but once she gave him a quick update, there were two mother fuckers ready to beat someone's ass. Much of Diamond's anguish was because Sasha was like a little sister to him, and he once had a crush on her. Therefore, it became very personal, and he was on board to do whatever.

Suddenly, Diamond jumped up and headed in the direction where Blaze and his date were seated. Once he got to the table, he immediately complimented the woman's dress and also complimented Blaze on how good they both looked together. Compliments never go out of style, especially when you are complimenting someone who lives for it. A good-looking man can charm the panties off a nun and the pick fork away from a devil. Once Diamond got back to the table, all their suspicions were confirmed: they were indeed an item and very much in love. As a matter of fact, they were at the "Sugar Bar" celebrating their second anniversary. No, they were not married but very much engaged. So, Suki was right; Blaze is not the man he wants many of them to believe. Although Kelis was never fooled, she was pissed because she gave him a chance to come clean, but he still continued to lie.

Suddenly, the room wasn't big enough for them all, especially Big Foot. She thought about confronting him but knew she needed to get more proof. Exposing Blaze this way was not going to be enough to convince Sasha. These days, her girl's head is so far in the clouds, it was going to take more than just two people having drinks in a bar to convince her otherwise. Flying on all cylinders, Kelis decided to call the one person she knew would get this party started... Suki! Just the mere mentioning of Blaze's name, the fool was on the first thing smoking... the 4 train.

While waiting for Suki to arrive, Kelis begins to second guess her decision about involving him since he, too, had personal feelings connected to this man. This was already a complicated situation, and he was not needed to make shit crazier. The end was near, but the heartbreak was just about to get started. This was not a girl-on-girl crime, where it's a fair fight amongst ladies. The relationship was unbalanced, unfair and unraveling. The realization is, no woman in the world could compete with a man's desire for a penis, so ladies, please do not even try.

An hour had passed, and Kelis had become very impatient. She and Diamond had moved the car out of the Sugar bars parking space to the parking garage across the street. Sitting in a 32-dollar-an-hour parking lot waiting for Suki to come from Brooklyn, was the last place they wanted to be.

Three more hours had passed and just when Diamond and Kelis were about to pull out, Suki called. Instead of calling when he arrived, he took matters into his own hands and did his own investigation. Just like Kelis imagined, this fool went off the script and did shit his way. So anxious to know what he did or said, she gave him a minute to get his ass across the street, where they were located.

When 30 minutes had passed, she and Diamond rode out of the garage. Kelis was furious, while the car was still in motion, she jumped out and stormed into the supper club. At this point, she couldn't care less who recognized her or what plan was blown. Once she rushed in, she spotted a saddened-looking Suki seated in the corner of the bar. He was nursing two drinks and informed Kelis that Blaze and his date had already left. What Kelis did not understand was the mood Suki was in and considered it to be a red flag. Not necessarily knowing what happened, she knew he was up to something and walked out nonchalantly. The ride home was quiet but interrupted by Suki insisting Diamond drop him by the MAC store before hitting the highway. That was the only normal Suki behavior he presented going home that evening. He was as quiet as a mouse, and that is not Suki.

CHAPTER 13

END OF A FRIENDSHIP

I has been almost a week and Suki has gone missing. Not the kind of disappearance that needs to be reported, but one that makes you wonder where he is. The situation about Blaze and the transgender has been put on hold. Kelis has been so busy trying to take care of her mom and making money she is almost on the verge of saying fuck it. Those all-night card games were beginning to wreak havoc on her sleep mode and her don't give-a fuck mode was heightened. Delaying the matter was a big mistake, but there was no need to cry over spilled milk. To get a better perspective about last week, she decided to give Suki a call. Multiple calls have been made, but none have been answered. She was now getting worried about the not answering the phone more than him not being seen. Trying to make sense of his disappearance, Kelis decided to play detective and researched his steps. The last time he was seen was when they dropped him off at the condo, and ever since that day, Sasha said he had not come back. Leonardo was the first person Kelis contacted and he thought Suki was staying at the condo in one of his moods. Pieces of the puzzle were coming together, especially once Sasha admitted that she had not seen Blaze in a few days either. It does not take Perry Mason to crack this case, and to make matters worse, Leonardo has been blowing up Kelis's phone, worrying about this fool. This is what Kelis did not want to happen... people worried about him, and he could be luxuriating at a spa. Until further notice, she had no other choice but to go about her business, which was going to check on her mom.

Ever since her last emotional breakdown, Kelis has made it her business to spend more time with her. The new medication prescribed seems to be working and her sleep pattern has improved. She has been communicating much better, and she has developed a heartier appetite. Kelis's work schedule was brutal, but she was going to make time to be with her mother, even if it was just for a 15-minute nap. (NEVER MEASURE THE AMOUNT OF TIME SPENT, MEASURE THE MOMENTS IN TIME) Also... sleeping next to a loved one is spiritual. In its moment, both parties are close to death.

While driving over the bridge, she got an unexpected call from Bleu. He had just gotten back in town and was desperate to see her. Bleu's urgencies are no longer Kelis's, but it has been about four months since he has been between her legs. Hooking up tonight was all his idea, but now that she has heard his voice, her body started responding, He must have picked up on her vibe because she was definitely up to some company tonight. Yes, his timing was on point, but he better be on time and bring something expensive to unwrap except his dick. Bleu was like a woman when it came to being on time. His clock is designed to benefit him, and this is why he and Kelis always seemed to clash.

Once she was done spending time with her mother, she headed back to the condo. Not knowing what time Bleu was going to finally make his appearance, she took a much-needed bath to wash away the day. Working at the club tonight is going to be long, considering she would be a solo act. Without a mere mention, the housekeeper had revved up the jacuzzi. Her name was (Patra), and she was sent from Heaven. Patra was more than a housekeeper; she was the gatekeeper to their souls. She did her job way above the call of duty while studying their personal habits. In some ways, she knew them more than they knew themselves. For starters, the jacuzzi temperature was always to Kelis's liking, just like the kind of champagne.

Not only was the condo always impeccably cleaned, but she also kept their personal belongings in order. She kept a calendar marking their periods, so there would always be Tampons and 800 mil Ibuprofens. Their personals things were kept more stocked than at Targets. She was so sweet and considerate, and you could not ask for better help if a genie granted you one wish. While soaking in the jacuzzi of warm bubbles, the scented candles gave the bathroom its Ambience. The funky sound of Fantasia piped through the heated marble floors. Kelis was in her own world and Bleu was anywhere but soaking next to her.

Suddenly, Kelis started touching her breast, and the feeling was sensational. She then slowly reached down between her legs and started vigorously massaging her clitoris. The feeling was so sensational and in that moment a man was not needed, just wanted. So in-depth of pleasuring herself, she never heard a sound. Out of nowhere, a deep voice said, "I'll be taking over from here, it was Bleu." She looked up at him unstartled and continued on. As she moaned and groaned, his eyes widened while his penis thickened. Suddenly, he wanted what she was delivering, so he began taking off his clothes. While he began undressing, she lost focus on herself, and all her attention was on him. Standing naked in her bathroom was a superb, chiseled body carved straight from any tree in Africa. He entered the Jacuzzi with two bottles of "Ace of Spade" champagne. One for their palate and the other was poured down her chest, through her legs and clitoris. Her locked heart got away from her, and it was beating rapidly.

Throughout their evening, she questioned him how he was able to enter the condo unannounced and he joked that he had climbed the walls. Bleu was a lot of things, but Spiderman, he was not. But if compared to any action hero Black Panther, yes! He was strong, although the thought of him climbing walls was possible, considering the way he just entered hers. After a nice blunt was smoked, the minor bickering simmered. Repeatedly he continued and she followed. To watch Bleu rolled a blunt is so fucking sexy. He licks it, like he licks a pussy. After multiple blunts were smoked and bottles of champagne were drunk, they were at it again. More champagne was brought to the room and most of it was poured on her body rather than down their throats. To have cold champagne sipped off someone's warm body is the freakiest shit ever. Any man could eat a pussy with or without toppings, but a pussy soaked in champagne is a delicacy. Kelis was in her glory while her legs were wrapped around his head. When it was all over, water was everywhere, as if it were a tsunami. Knowing that the day was about to end, she spent the rest of the evening, wrapped in his arms.

Two hours into her ecstasy nap, she got an unexpected call from Diamond. When she recognized the number, she immediately answered the phone. Diamond was at the Marriot Hotel downtown having drinks when he spotted Suki in the hotel coming off the elevator. He was fabulously dressed as usual but was seen alone. According to how he was walking and talking, Suki was indeed intoxicated… but what else was new? Not knowing if it was a good idea to approach him, Diamond decided to observe him from afar. Turns out Suki was staying at the hotel with a mystery guest. Having to deal with Bleu's unexpected visit and Suki's disappearance, Kelis was capped with emotions. Not knowing how to make sense of the information, she hung up on Diamond and began to think.

Hours had passed and she was no longer in the "Land of make-believe. Cinderella was back from the ball, wearing nothing but a black satin thong and a diamond belly chain. Every unpleasant thought surfaced in her mind, but it was time to make the donuts. Unsurprisingly, Diamond called back, and this time, he demanded that she meet him at the hotel ASAP! Diamond understood the importance of Keli's job but knew she needed to talk to Suki. After she got the clearance from Lexus to cover her shift, there were green lights all the way.

When she arrived, Diamond was pacing back and forth in front of the hotel like a madman. By the look on his face, she knew something really unsettling had pissed him off. Diamond was a very busy man, and his time was precious and profitable. Unfortunately, Kelis had no other choice but to recruit him because, if trusted by anyone else, their business would make the papers. Once she got up on him, he firmly grabbed her hand and quickly ushered her into the side door of the hotel. Diamond was a well-traveler and had stayed in thousands of dollars per night suites. Although the Marriott was a nice place, it did not compare to the many hotels he visited. Back in the day, the Marriott was the shits, but it does not compare to the Waldorf Astoria. He and the owner's sister were long-time business associates. LOL… that is just another way to say he was servicing her, too, for a fee. That bitch was crazy; she had access to 200 free rooms at her brother's hotel but instead paid three times the amount to get fucked somewhere else.

Diamond's attitude escalated because she gave us information on Suki and his stay there, and she was exchanging that info for some dick. Diamond was pissed but did it out of love for Kelis. She orchestrated the hotel personnel to give us information on Suki's whereabouts and even gave us access to the key to his room. One call to the front desk and Suki's itinerary was detailed. He was staying on the fourth floor, room 403. The room was registered to Donald Peterson aka John Doe! They ordered hot wings, strawberries, and Corona beer from room service. Donald Peterson had checked in at 4 o'clock and was checking out tomorrow by noon. The information was informative but inconclusive because we knew Suki, but who was Donald Peterson? Numerous calls to the room were made and a "Do Not Disturb" sign was hung on the door. The entire hotel staff was put on notice and because guests have rights, this matter had to be handled carefully, or whoever in that room besides Suki could have a lawsuit. To avoid any mishaps or unruliness, Kelis and Diamond decided that they were going to take full responsibility for any way this situation unfolded.

Once they reached the fourth floor, somehow, the reality of invading someone's privacy did not sit well with Kelis. According to how she was raised, a person's privacy was honored but this was Suki, a man who shows up always unannounced and never calls before he comes. As they exited the staircase, room 403 was further down the hall. Once she collected her breath, she and Diamond banged on the door like the police and still, nobody answered. An unanswered door was what they expected, but with help from a cute little surveillance camera, Suki had entered the room three hours ago with a gentleman in black shades and a hoodie. The first knock was preliminary; the second was for those who were looking, and there was no need for the third; they were going in with the hotel key. Once the door opened, they slowly but cautiously walked in. The room was filled with citrus candles and fully bloomed long-stemmed pink roses... yes, Suki was here. In the far corner of the room, sitting on the bed facing the window, was no surprise the man with Suki on the surveillance camera. In-person, he had a long torso with broad shoulders, something the camera didn't reveal.

Immediately after entering, Kelis apologized to him for their improper evasion. Slowly, the guy stood up and around, and Kelis's mouth dropped; it was Blaze. This time, he did not appear embarrassed but somewhat relieved. Finally, some answers were about to be answered, but the most important question was, "Where is Suki and why are you two here together?" To not be so dead on, Kelis asked questions to answer what she already knew. As much as she had waited for this day to come, now that it had arrived, she was not ready for it. Her hatred towards Blaze was no longer that serious, but her concerns for her two best friends were! Right now, Kelis was so confused and angry and could not understand how he and Blaze were back fucking around? According to the surveillance cameras, Suki was still in the room, but Blaze did not know they had access to the cameras. Even without the cameras, Suki's things and DNA were all over the room and a closed bathroom door gave them confirmation that he was hiding.

While Kelis was interrogating Blaze, Diamond asked to use the bathroom, and the look on Blaze's face, he knew we were on to them. When they tried to open the bathroom door, it was locked, so Kelis tried to tear the door off the hinges. She continued to knock and kick until finally, Blaze convinced Kelis to let him into the bathroom to talk to Suki. She also had to promise them that once the door opened, she would not burst in. At that point, Kelis was not in the mood to compromise with Blaze but knew he was the only one that stupid mother fucker would listen to at this point.

When the door opened for Blaze to enter, she had intentions of pushing her way in but realized how much influence that man obviously had over him. Time was of the essence, and so was Kelis's patience. Then suddenly, they both exited the bathroom, holding hands. It was something out of "West Side Story," two lovers torn by a misunderstanding … SMMFH! The sight of them made her want to throw up, and to top it off, her newly manicured nails were fucked up. There they stood, looking like they were about to board a plane to their honeymoon destination, while Kelis stood drenched in sweat. As the two misfortunate lovers huddled, Kelis made it her business to intervene. She was all for love for those who believed in it, but this was not going to be a "happy ever after" ending for us all.

Kelis waited patiently for Suki's explanation and didn't need Blaze to cosign. Still shivering like a puppy, left out in the cold, he started by saying that he intended to expose Blaze, but once they both got alone together, the universe shifted. Whatever divided them years ago was an amicable decision, but once they crossed paths at his birthday party, something had reawakened in both of them. Blaze admitted that since that day, he couldn't get Suki off his mind and knew that he had to tell Sasha. Once he saw him again at the "Sugar Bar," he was more convinced that he could no longer live this lie.

Once both of their truths were told, Kelis unexpectedly understood their dilemma. Unfortunately, Sasha was her friend, and her broken heart was her only concern. There at the hotel many questions were answered, but the story here was…who is going to tell her and how will all of this affect her? The idea of a man struggling with his sexual identity or any issues, bears no concern to Kelis. Personally, she's heartless about the matter and just the thought of a mother fucker sticking his peanut butter in her jelly blows hers. In life, there are choices, and it's either left or right, black or white. The same as when choosing what sex you prefer, Adam & Eve or Adam & Steve. Either way, CHOOSE MOTHER FUCKER!

CHAPTER 14

AUNT LEXUS LEAVES TOWN

It has been confirmed that a generous offer for the house was being highly considered. Once upon a time, their home was nearly falling apart, and serious renovation was needed. The cost was tremendously high, and in order to fund the project, her grandmother had to pour a lot of drinks and cut a lot of games. Times were very hard, and once Kelis's grandfather died; her grandmother became a widower at 30 years old. She was young and very naïve and knew nothing about the game or the streets. She came from a time when men took care of their families, and a woman's job was to take care of the children and keep the house. Today, women are liberated and very independent, mostly because they have to be. Many men have abandoned their families and women have had to go to work in order to feed their babies. Keeping that in mind, since welfare was not an option, Kelis's grandmother used her culinary talent and started selling dinners from her home. Since playing cards and drinking were their favorite pastime, it was no wonder she knew how to profit from it. Kelis's grandmother was a true hustler, and since her passing, many of her old friends and business partners still come through to pay homage.

Amongst the group were well-wishers but many were vultures that only came to pick over her remains. While growing up, Kelis sat courtside and overheard and viewed a lot of very unpleasant activities. Many of the gangsters played on their team, but they were cold killers. To overhear a man say he killed his best friend for fucking his wife was mind-blowing, but to hear someone say they killed a human being for just stepping on his shoes is horrendous. As Kelis has gotten older, she no longer fears any of them, mostly since most of them are dead or in jail. LET THE RECORD BE SHOWN: Her home wasn't anything like the Huxtables and she was no way like Denise or Rudy. Nowadays, a lot of time is being spent reminiscing and holding on to bad memories. Wanting to depart from your old life and start over is understandable, but making hasty decisions about selling the only valuable and monumental thing you ever owned is not wise. The proceeds may appear to be the financial boost needed, but once that money is gone, what do they have left?

Although she was not in the habit of counting anyone's coins, her grandmother left them financially straight. If anything, Porsche has a better head start since she's planning on moving to Chicago. Chicago is where her father was raised, and he has lots of family still residing there. From what Kelis was told, they were a little crazy and considered modern-day Hillbillies. Long ago, before her grandfather's death, the crew from Chicago came to Brooklyn for a family reunion. While at the reunion, a game of cards broke out. First, they played spades, then poker, next Pity Pat. Everyone knows plenty of smack is often talked at any card game but when you're playing for money, the words can be more intense. Uncle William, which is Kelis's grandfather's oldest brother, after a long day of sipping moonshine, decided to join in at the pity pat table.

Everyone knows some of the worst alcoholics cannot drink moonshine, but Uncle William was true to the concoction. Buzzed like a bee, many were very reluctant to let him play, but once those dead presidents made an appearance, a hush was heard over the crowd. With much hesitation coming from the direction of the wise, it was just a matter of time before things got ugly. In the beginning, Uncle William was obeying the rules and pretty much-kicking ass. Beginner's luck is what it's called. Two hours in, his luck, disposition and plenty of cards were changed. Kelis's grandfather knew where all this was headed and demanded his brother part ways from the table. Just like any intoxicated fool who doesn't know how to hold their liquor or lose, turn a good thing into bad. Uncle William was furious and demanded his money, but we all know that isn't about to happen. The rules of the game do not apply to Uncle William since he lives according to his own. We are talking about a man who lives like a mountaineer, and moonshine is not something he loves to drink, it's something he cannot do without.

Once the commotion got under control, everyone kept their eyes on Uncle William. Sitting in the corner still fumigating and sipping that mad juice, Uncle William was still speaking out of turn about money he lost fairly. Disturbing words were coming from the table and all sides of the room. Uncle William was truly a crazy mother fucker and brags about shooting deer for sport back home. What he does not know is, niggas in Brooklyn shoot people, for sport. Suddenly, the commotion escalated again, and this time, in order to shut his brother up, Kelis's grandfather had to put his oldest brother in a serious chokehold. Considering Kelis's family's reputation, Uncle William would have been beheaded long before the clock struck midnight. It took a lot of convincing and almost a tranquilizer to calm him down.

For the rest of the night, Uncle William sat quietly in the corner of the room, sipping his devil's brew. He was so heavily guarded and was not even allowed to blink his eyes. While contained, silence absorbed the room.

Then, when everything finally got quiet and nobody was looking, Uncle William pulled out a gun from his boot and shot through the room. Everyone hit the floor and pandemonium broke out. All of the family, along with some outsiders, ran for their lives. The only ones that remained in the room were Kelis's grandfather and Big Whiz. They were from the streets and the sound of gunshots was like listening to a melody. After the smoke cleared and all the family was OK, there was one casualty… Pacquiao. Pacquiao was Dominican and his family sold the best heroin in Brooklyn. The Pacquiao family owned plenty of foreign cars, and Kelis's grandfather did lots of repairs on their cars in his shop.

Everyone was ordered out of the house, and her grandfather and Big Whiz handled shit. Calls were made to some heavy hitters and the body was removed to an undisclosed place. All of the family and a few outsiders knew not to ever mutter a word about what took place at the house that night. Unfortunately, the streets started talking and that kind of talk wasn't good for business or their welfare. Kelis's grandfather had a good reputation with people, but his occasional interactions with a few gangsters had many questioning his truth. Joseph's brother William has always been crazy, but he was family. Family or not, Joseph ordered his only brother to leave his home and never return. Over the years, the family from Chicago felt Kelis's grandfather had taken sides, and that created the tension that divided them. Joseph and William never spoke again and most of those involved passed on. The new generation wanted no part of the old generation's curses and was willing to right the wrongs of their kin folk.

After Joseph's death, his brother continued to stay in seclusion, and bitterness and moonshine destroyed his mind. When he died, he left a big house to their baby sister, Rose. It took a lot of money to renovate the home, but it was something Rose wanted to do. Rose was the only girl in their family and was loved and adored. She had a striking resemblance to their mother, whom the two brothers cherished. Lexus also carried that same gene, and she looks exactly like their mother and sister. When Rose heard that Lexus was coming to Chicago to study medicine, she offered her to stay at the house rent-free for as long as she needed. That gesture was the final pledge in rebuilding that bridge that was torn down so drastically.

Lexus's bags were packed for weeks, and all that was left on the agenda was to say goodbye. Kelis painfully wanted to neglect the day when her aunt would depart but knew she had to embrace it. She also knew that she would now have to solely deal with Porsche and the business, but the original deed found in her mother's closet would be her safety net. Everyone knows Porsche is a handful, but they're both the same species; one just scratches a little harder than the other.

The day has finally arrived, and her swollen eyes and tear-soaked pillow have all the evidence of a broken heart. Lexus left for Chicago on an 8:45 am flight. Her last-minute calls from the airport went unanswered because saying goodbye isn't always easy. Instead, Kelis used the time in solitude to reminisce, and many of their conversations played over in her head. Her aunt's final say was that leaving her behind was not an easy task and that she was not abandoning a child but a strong, grown-ass woman. She also hopes she keeps an eye on Porsche, and normally, that wouldn't be a problem, but Kelis had already had her hands full with taking care of her mother. The caretaker's button was now once again pinned on her shirt without her permission. She was always someone they needed to keep a close eye on, but Kelis was not about to make Porsche her obligation. They were family, and the only thing they had left in common was the club. Kelis's poker face has many of them fooled. Although she appears incredibly strong, she is beaten and broken. Her beautiful exterior covers all the cracks and bruises in her heart. Therefore, the weight of the world was beginning to weigh heavily, and she had so little fight left in her.

PS. THE RAGING BATTLE CONTINUES AND HER HARDEST FIGHT WAS HER GAMBLING ADDICTION AND RIGHT NOW, IT WAS WINNING!

CHAPTER 15

PORSCHE'S BREAKDOWN

Have you ever heard of the saying, a man cannot turn a hoe into a housewife but will leave his housewife for a hoe? Mr. Tyson did an unbelievable thing and indeed left his wife. He stands on a noticeably short list of men that really choose their side bitch over their wife. Since his return, Porsche has devoted a lot of her time to him and has kept her hoeing to a minimum. Throughout the years, she has been sneaking around with this old dude, but I guess the luster has vanished when there are no longer reasons to hide anymore. Turns out, he did not leave his wife; she got rid of his ass. She finally got tired of his bullshit, multiple outside babies and STDs. She eventually lawyered up and divorced him. DNA testing was not needed since all of his children had the same big head as he had. All his wife's demands were met, and he walked away from the marriage with merely enough to buy coffee.

When he arrived at Porsche's doorsteps, he had his duffle bag filled with more lies and promises. However, Porsche had a bag of her own, filled with the same essentials. Mr. Tyson had a hold on Porsche, and even though she fooled around with many others, she preserved him differently. Was it the age difference or the fact that he was not always available? Whatever it was, she was a tiger, but in his presence, she mellowed down to a kitten. It's funny how everyone has that one person that they cannot shake, and all the scientific analogies can't draw any conclusions, like Cleopatra and Caesar or Popeye and Olive Oyl.

The crowd at the club was changing and so were the times. Men were demanding not only strippers but bitches who knew how to really dance. Not only were the men making noise, but the women at the club also wanted to see a booty clap for obvious reasons. More bisexual women were gambling, and they were not camouflaged in baggy jeans and a doo rag. They were fine bitches that liked to get their clit licked more than their pussy dicked. When it came to hiring strippers, the job was not an easy task. Kelis needed a chick with not just a bad body and a pretty face. She wanted someone who took their job seriously and had good hygiene. One thing Kelis could not tolerate was a nasty house or woman. The theory that most strippers are drug addicted women or runaways is undisputedly true, but Kelis auditioned many women who were just working to make a living. Some did it to feed their babies, while many were doing it to pay for college. She interviewed many that did it because it was a now thing and just wanted to be part of the movement. She believed in equal opportunity employment, but she was a perfectionist and believed strippers needed to be perfect. Therefore, she wanted girls that had no dimples on their thighs, stretch marks or red eyes. A stripper is supposed to be a man or woman's fantasy, and, in our fantasies, there are no blemishes.

Ms. Remsen has been coming by the club lately to say hello. She occasionally abandons her post in the window, but she will not be gone for long. Some nights, if the club were at its busiest, she would stick around to help. Her presence is always accepted since she is the best security system to have on deck. Occasionally, on the nights that Porsche works, Kelis pays Ms. Remsen to be her eyes. Ms. Remsen is now in her early eighties, and her eyes aren't as good as they once were due to cataracts. Cataract to a nosey old broad like Ms. Remsen is like someone cutting a couple of fingers from Liberace's hands. Banged up and all, she is an old, trusted friend of Kelis's grandmother, and she would trust her with her life. Since time has the best of Ms. Remsen, she rolls with her granddaughters most days. They were from North Carolina and used to visit every summer to spend time with her. They are now grown up and out and have no plans on leaving NY. They always loved Brooklyn and have always vowed to stay one day, but Brooklyn is not reared for us all. They were here for the bright lights of Broadway and the long night of the clubs. They were country girls with strong accents and big asses. Their presence at the club had Porsche hairs rising, along with many dicks. I do not know what annoyed Porsche more, Ms. Remsen spying or that she brought along a string of stallions to the rodeo. Ms. Remsen's granddaughters were strangers to many but not to Kelis's family.

Ms. Remsen's had a daughter name (Charity). She was 13 years old when she gave birth to her. Back then an unwed mother and in this case an unwed child was highly embarrassing. Ms. Remsen's parents took her to New York to a family member's home. There at her mother's sister's house, she gave birth to a baby girl (Charity). The family adopted the child and Ms. Remsen was sent away to an undisclosed place. Over the years Ms. Remsen never got over them, taking her child away but eventually settled into a fairly decent life. Once both her parents died, Ms. Remsen decided to tell her only child the truth. So, since her daughter discovered the truth, she used every bit of the situation to her advantage and always made her feel guilty about not raising her. Therefore, Ms. Remsen allowed guilt to overcome her and did whatever it took to make it up to her daughter and, later, her children.

Mercedes and Charity were two years apart, so they were more familiar with one another. However, Porsche and Lexus were a little younger, so their memory was not as vague. Regardless of how it begins or ends, Ms. Remsen was like family to their mother, so that made her family to them all. Porsche was always on high alert when other bitches were around, especially since Mr. Tyson had claimed the corner seat at the end of the bar. At some point, all women have insecurities, but confidence can dead those emotions. Porsche was nothing to reckon with, when it came to looks but a youthful candle shine brighter.

Ms. Remsen had a granddaughter; her name was Serenity. She was a pretty girl with a sweet southern accent. She came with no instructions and had Mr. Tyson's attention. Being an army man, he was used to such discipline, but this girl was the type to make an officer AWOL. A lot of men gave into that sweet, naïve, innocent disposition, thinking she would be easy to mold and control. But what they did not know was that Serenity was putting on an act, and her clay was not for molding. She had the kind of game Kelis respected and believed at another time or place; they could have been friends.

To eliminate the competition, Porsche barred Mr. Tyson from the club. Moving onto greener pastures was OK with him because he was now free to do whatever he wanted elsewhere. He was a man about his business and did not care where he drank, just as long as the drinks weren't watered down or spiked. Oh, what a dumb move on her part, sending him to spend money at another establishment and also giving him the freedom to be with other women. That stinking thinking is what separated the two, so no longer was Mr. Tyson seated at their bar or table. He was now spending hundreds of dollars nightly somewhere else. He was the money man, and nobody knew that better than the young ladies at the club. Women like Porsche want to believe that they are the only younger woman their man ever had. Normally, when an older dude dates a younger woman, that's all he usually dates. Once he gets a naïve bitch to do what he wants, there is no way he is going to want to entertain a confident intelligent one. The game Serenity was playing is not effective to a man who knows how to play her game. Men like Mr. Tyson go along to get along. He was not interested in trying to mold, control or wife anyone at the time. He wanted some new young pussy, and if that pussy told him to bark like a dog, he would have. The streets were always talking, and the newfound gossip was that Serenity and Mr. Tyson had become an item. Along with them being a happy twosome, some say he was now living with her at her grandmother's house (Ms. Remsen).

Kelis was big on loyalty and Ms. Remsen was considered family, but that kind of shit separated how she felt about her. When those girls came from North Carolina, they were considered family. She remembers as a young child, how her grandmother allowed them the same luxury as she had given her own kids. When they all got of age, her grandmother and Ms. Remsen always said... you girls play fair, and under any circumstances, never share the same sausage. Along with never going against the family was her grandmother's biggest rule. Today many women don't have a problem sharing the same dick but to Kelis if so, you might as well wear the same underwear. Those were defined rules to live by, but I guess those rules do not apply to everyone. They say karma is a bitch, and although Kelis would not want to admit it, Porsche fucked a few young guys she once dated.

It was a Friday night and Porsche was scheduled to work but somehow could not get out of bed. This had been the third time this month that Kelis had to cover for her. Kelis was no stranger to long hours, but long hours were beginning to wreak havoc on her body. Porsche was beginning to drink a lot and at other bars in hopes of catching Mr. Tyson with their so-called family member. So, one morning, after working at the club all night, Kelis went to Porsche's room to check in on her. After about three knocks, nobody answered, and that is when Kelis took it beyond herself and walked in.

When she entered the room, Porsche was face down in vomit. At first, she thought it was another drunken episode and profusely started cursing her out, but it turns out Porsche was really sick. Kelis asked her if she had the flu and she said no. Many other suggestions were tossed up, but Porsche stopped her in her tracks and told her that she was pregnant. Kelis stood stunned because Porsche was also a birth control advocate. "How could this happen?" Kelis said with her head down. She admitted that with all that was going on, some days she was forgetting to take her birth control pills. Kelis was hip to the shit because everyone knows when you stop taking the pill, you start bleeding. Porsche knew Kelis knew the score and admitted that she purposely stopped taking the pill in order to get pregnant. Kelis always thought her aunt was a bit clueless but did not know to what degree.

A brief conversation was had and then Kelis helped Porsche into the shower. While in the shower, the conversation was revisited. Kelis told Porsche that getting pregnant does not help a woman keep a man but has all the ingredients to make a mother fucker bounce. Porsche has had her share of so many men, but for some reason, this old dude has her in a trance. After marinating her pregnancy for the next two months, she finally told Mr.

Tyson. News of her pregnancy did not make him run out and buy cigars. He was not a happy man and why should he? He had already fathered seven children, two with his wife and five others from women he met while in the service, traveling all over the world.

By the time Porsche was almost six months, Serenity was also pregnant too. During this time, she and Mr. Tyson had gone their separate ways, and she was prepared to raise the child alone. Then, one night, Serenity came into their business with some friends sporting a tiny bump. First on the mind of those in charge... who let her in and when is she and her herd of cows leaving? Believing that you never let them see you sweat, Kelis demanded that Porsche stay cool and unaffected. Whatever point those bitches were trying to make, backed fired. As long as they were buying drinks, they were absolute to those they were trying to impress.

Later that night, Porsche told Kelis that seeing Serenity pregnant also, was crazy. The thought of sharing the same man was not as horrifying as almost sharing the same due date. Come that morning, Porsche had decided to look into a late-term abortion. An Abortion is an abortion, but anything after its first trimester, Kelis and many others consider murder. However, it's a woman's choice, but a man's departure should never determine it. If so, that's heartbreaking, and no man should be given that much power. Fortunately, God had the last word, and just when an appointment was made, she miscarried. Although she had planned on terminating the pregnancy, the miscarriage was unexpected and devastating. During that time, she learned that she loved her baby and began to love something else other than Mr. Tyson... herself.

Six months later, she found out that Serenity had given birth to a bouncing baby boy, and she and Mr. Tyson had gotten married. Holy Shit... pigs do fly... some men do marry their jump-off! I guess she was the one or the one left standing. News of their prenuptial hit home and an invitation was sent to the house. A bigger woman would accept, but when you cut ties with family, there is no revisiting anything... not even sometimes going to their funerals. Too bad Ms. Remsen was part of the deal, but she was guilty by association. Unlike words spoken by the "GODFATHER."

IT WAS BUSINESS AND PERSONAL!

CHAPTER 16

TURNING 25

Come this Friday, Kelis will be turning 25 years old. All birthdays are welcoming, but there is something about a girl turning 25! She's more than grown and still excitedly considered a very young woman. Surprisingly, no plans were made, but you best believe something fabulous was on the horizon.

Kelis was always done with the best birthdays, from her very first to the previous. Every year, it was getting harder & harder to outdo the year before. No matter how grand or beautiful, the night always ends in gambling. Much of the fanfare has stayed the same, but the number of people in her inner circle has changed. A room filled with fake people handing out fake wishes was not what she now considered a great celebration. Many times, the birthday person normally celebrates according to other people's wishes and ideas.

Since Kelis was not in search of a theme, she was more open to doing something different. Therefore, since the last decade of her life had been very tumultuous and predictable, she had thought of maybe going away for her birthday. She was not an experienced traveler and all she ever really wanted to go was to Atlantic City or Vegas. However, she has been to other fascinating places in her life but none that required a passport. Sometimes, our environment can stunt our growth and make barbed wire look like a picket fence. When all you know is the block, the block afterwhile becomes cemented walls. When it comes to traveling, most of our people think going to Jamaica or the Bahamas is the ultimate vacation. There is nothing wrong with traveling to such destinations, but how many sandy beaches and watered-down drinks should one person endure? Come next vacation, same shit, different Island. It seems to me that people travel just to be somewhere, but really, they haven't been anywhere. Also, Kelis wasn't a beachy girl, and after she has flaunted her body, and got way too much sand in her hair, she will be ready to trade those flip flops in for a pair of red bottoms. She was a city girl, and her feet were more comfortable walking on cement. Also, wherever she went, a casino had to be near, and those islands casinos sucked. There are never any big winners and if there are any, they're often found missing... LOL!

Anywhere she went, gambling had to be on the menu because it kept her adrenaline just where it needed to be... at a thousand. So, that being said, there would be just enough sand between her toes but plenty of Henny poured down her throat. All the ingredients to bake the perfect vacation at 370-degrees. If she was going to go to Vegas, she was going to keep the excursion a secret.

Just recently, Suki had put a bug in her ear about Bleu wanting to surprise her for a weekend getaway. He entrusted the one fool that cannot hold anything in his mouth but a dick. Nevertheless, Kelis was not upset about the surprise being exposed because Suki knew better than to keep anything concerning Bleu to himself. If only Bleu knew that "space" in a beautiful box would be the ultimate gift. Going away for a romantic weekend or having an elaborate party no longer thrilled her. One thing she had learned from Sasha and Suki's fiasco is that being honest with people, not only is best but it only benefits the liar.

To be honest, the club was making good money but because of her gambling addiction, and Porsche being on a temporary hiatus, she was faced with some serious money troubles. Her recent plans to increase their revenue have not been going accordingly as planned. On paper, the numbers were there but not the money. Nothing was going right for Kelis, and mostly because she refused to admit what the problem was. Everyone's life to her seemed to be progressing, and everything she was trying to do to get ahead was not happening. Bills collectors were threatening and so was some of the people that came to the club. Desperately she has been contemplating going to Bleu for a loan, but going to him would be worse than going to any bank or loan shark. Although he wouldn't charge Kelis with any interest, she would have to pay with her soul. He was the perfect and most reliable one to go to but, those… I told you so's would kill her. If only in her dreams, she could go to him for the money, he would give it to her without any back talk. She thought they both were committed to a no strings attached relationship, with respect and cash flow always given, along with giving him the best pussy a man could receive. To her that was the perfect game plan, but Bleu had so much more to give her, because he loved her, and she knew it.

Upon all her newfound interest, she wanted to openly date other men maybe some from other races. Black men will always be her thing, but most of the brothers, especially the ones there in Brooklyn, weren't about shit. They were all into chasing manufactured bitches and no longer appreciated women that were born naturally small at the waist and cute in the face! They were also in the habit of demanding more and giving less. However, her taste buds were changing, and she was dying to try other flavors.

As the day loomed, her final stop was to Suki's apartment. It was Labor

Day weekend, and the temperature was at its highest. Suki was now living with Blaze in a beautiful, expensive apartment in Prospect Heights. He had invited Kelis over to his home for a seafood luncheon for her birthday. Their apartment was decorated so beautifully and smelled so clean. How is it that gay men keep the cleanest homes while the average male or female don't even make their beds daily. When Suki invites you to his house, it is such an experience. He knows how to entertain and make you feel so comfortable. He greets you with a smile, a cocktail, and slippers. There will be no walking around in dirty shoes that have been worn in the streets. Upon entry, he had three of the cutest Dalmatian puppies that also greeted you. His dogs meant everything to him, and if they picked up any bad energy, you would not be allowed to come into his home. Dogs have the most distinctive instincts if only humans did too. The smell of sea breeze addressed your nostrils, and your eyes were doused with a tastefully decorated black and white décor. To complement its color, red roses were collectively gathered on the nearest tables, and matching red leashes were worn around the dogs' necks. To not be overlooked, Suki's bright red lipstick and nail polish were not to be ignored. Listed on the menu were crab cakes, grilled corn, lobster salad, and Henny Coladas, while the sound of Kem drowned their ear lobes. The first Colada went down easy and was too freaking sweet, so after that, it was strictly Henny, no chaser.

After lunch, Blaze bid goodbye and that is when the real party took flight. It was what a girl needed, two friends harmonizing, talking shit, and drinking straight out of the bottle. You know, you got to have much love for a mother fucker, when his lips are questionable, and lord knows where Suki puts his. One bottle down and another one was just cracked when Phyllis

Hyman entered the room... aka Suki, singing *(You Know Just How to Love Me)*. Just when he was done, Sylvester booted her out the door with *(You're My friend)*. What is it about? Every time someone gets drunk, they think they can sing or start crying. Suki was the crier, while Kelis became Beyoncé. Being under the influence, stories are often told and embellished, and also after listening to someone else's problem, you realize yours isn't that bad!

Darkness took over the sky, and Kelis still had no clue about tomorrow, but that was OK because tonight she was celebrating her birthday with one of her dearest friends... HAPPY BIRTHDAY KELIS!!!!!!

CHAPTER 17

AT ANY MEANS NECESSARY

There weren't many things Kelis regretted in her life. If so, she could narrow it down to one hand. One of her few regrets was taking a young boy under her wing and almost single-handedly almost destroying his family. Back in High School, she met a young boy named Darius Coleman. During that time, she and Sasha used to escort kids from their school for a fee in her father's Limo. It all started as a dare and turned out to be very profitable and the coolest thing since "New Edition." Most of the children were from their school, so that made the trips convenient. The back seat of the Limo is where many of the kids choose to play cards since many of them were afraid to cut class.

Everything was going cocoa butter smooth, until Darius Coleman Jr. entered her world. Darius was a spoiled rich kid with plenty of money but no personality. He was considered a cornball, so every afternoon after school, he would show up at Bay Ridge in hopes of making a friend or maybe finally meeting a girl. He was desperate to make friends and ready to purchase one at any cost. Those insecurities almost cost him his life and his trust fund. Darius was a permanent fixture outside of Bay Ridge once school led out. Since Bay Ridge was an all-girls school, he got no further than the school steps. One day, while everyone was piling into the Limo, Darius Coleman eased his slick ass into the back seat. Cocky as ever and oh so stupid, he thought he could get away with not being seen. Kelis noticed his big head in the back but did not say a word. The Limo service was for those who attended Bay Ridge, but with the kind of money Darius had, Kelis couldn't care less if he went to any school at all.

Months had gone by, and their car service business and the money made cutting games in the school bathroom had become very lucrative and popular. Just when the last hundred was counted, someone ratted them out. For a long time, Kelis couldn't figure out who blew the whistle until Darius' daddy made it clear. Just to think, it all started by playing for cigarettes and lunch passes. Then, one day, somebody threw a dollar on the bathroom floor. Not so long after that, the big prize was playing for homework and book reports. When someone knew how to forge report cards, all hell broke loose.

Every kid in the school wanted to be down, and about 70% of them were participating. Kelis was the ringleader, cutting those games and making money and enemies at the same time. Children were going home demanding more allowance and many cut notices were being sent home. After an investigation was made and an official statement from Darius, school officials had no choice but to expel Kelis and Sasha. Kelis made a strong case for herself, but everyone knew she was the brains behind the operation. Since the school year was almost over, the only feasible thing they decided to do was not to let them both attend their graduation. Not attending her high school graduation was fine with her, especially since there will be no one in her family most likely attending. Personally, all she wanted to do was grab her diploma and head for the door. Now Sasha, on the other hand, had a supportive cast and had plenty of people to disappoint.

Looking back on those days, the only memorable times were the gambling in the bathroom, the cafeteria lady and a couple of security guards. Thanks to the cafeteria lady for sneaking her as many chocolate chip cookies, she could eat and security for looking the other way as she snuck Suki in and out of the school. Furthermore, she hated school and couldn't wait to look at it in her rear-view mirror.

Once she ran into Darius at a mutual associate's cookout, Kelis was on a whole new, different vibe. She was no longer gambling for cigarettes or hanging out with kids her age. She was fucking men now and her gambling addiction was fucking her harder. By the end of the night, just when she was about to leave, Darius approached her by the curb. As she hoped her ride was fast approaching, she hoped more for Darius to state his case. He appeared quite nervous and the words from his mouth were just as shaken. He went on to say not much of anything but did apologize for how things went down long ago. Just when he was about to walk away, he turned and told her that much of the confusion was because he was pressured by his parents. What a difference a few years made? Darius was still obnoxious and cornier than ever and the only thing she still found interesting in him, was his money. In hopes of never seeing him again, she would, at various unforbidden places. Much of her knowledge seemed coincidental, but she later learned she was being stalked.

It was a Thursday evening, and she went to a dice game in Ditmars Park. It's been a while since she has played a game of dice but was told that plenty of money was going to be there. While strolling through the park, she ran into her stalker. He approached her with the same tired hello. When asked why he was there, he claimed to be hanging out with some friends. Kelis knew Darius was not there hanging but pretending. Darius's existence was a nonfactor, like always, so she continued on her journey.

It was now after 9 o'clock and the sunny park had gotten dark. Where they were playing, the lighting was not that bright due to the city's negligence. Dark or not, Kelis was rolling sixes, and they all didn't need much lighting to see that. Her luck was on, and it was like taking candy from a baby. She walked away from that dice game with eight thousand dollars and the guys she was playing with were pissed the fuck off. Not necessarily because they lost but most likely because she was a female. Five testosterones against one estrogen, was not what they believed or expected.

As she walked away, she stopped at the first tree she saw to put her money in her panties. Walking through the park, it dawned on her how dark it really was, so she started to put some heat to her steps. Just when she had gotten halfway out of the park, something with a heavy force came from behind and rustled her to the ground. She then began to fight back but realized she was up against something too powerful. Of course, she was outmatched; it was two guys. At first, she thought she was about to be raped by two strangers, but noticed they were two brothers she had just gambled with.

Once she realized she had no wins, she just stopped fighting and laid still. As one of them held her by the throat, the other guy rambled through her bag and then her pockets. When no money was found, his grip around her neck got tighter to the point where she almost couldn't breathe. They demanded the money and with little effort to talk, she told them it was in her underwear. Getting into Kelis's panties was always a joy to most men, and to think, these two were getting in without even buying her dinner. The one that was doing the searching could've grabbed the entire stash, but he decided to take what seemed like a dollar at a time. This way, he had the liberty to rub up against her pussy to retrieve it. Once they got the money, she continued to lay still on the ground, but the nightmare was far from over. The searcher seemed to have gotten an arousal and wanted more out of her panties. He then started to pull them down to her ankles and widen her legs open forcefully.

While she lay on the cold, nasty grass, she thought of all the times she had teased men with her pussy and now here is someone who is going to take it without permission. She was prepared to be raped and knew it was nothing she could do about it. She hoped it would be quick, but it turns out the piece of shit, did not want to rape her with his penis but with his tongue. He was fascinated by the way her pussy looked and smelled. Have you ever heard of such a thing? Although there was no penetrating, it was still considered rape. After he went on licking her completely from back to front, she closed her eyes and locked in the moment with prayer. Just when he was done, he looked like a salivating Rottweiler. So cold, angry, and scared, Kelis believed the worst was over, but his friend had other intentions.

During this time, Kelis had forgotten he had come with a partner. She was still laying on the ground when his accomplice came kneeling over her with his dick in his hand. He then asked her to get on her knees to suck his dick. That's when she knew she had to do something because she was not in the dick-sucking business. Just when the unthinkable was about to happen, she heard gunshots. Not knowing where the shots were coming from but knowing who was hit. Several feet away was the one that desperately needed to eat her pussy and the one that desired a blow job nearly stumbled on her when hit. So, shaken with fear, all Kelis could do was get up off her knees and run as fast as she could. Once she began to run, she ran right into Darius, standing not too far away, behind a tree, holding the smoking gun. Without question, they both ran out of the park, but not before she went back and got her money, their money, and the jewelry, they were wearing. Going back to the scene of the crime was a stupid move but satisfying. Kelis was not afraid of dead people. It's the live ones that frighten her.

After that day, Darius was granted his wish to be seen with Kelis, but there were still rules he needed to obey. Loyalty was one of her biggest pet peas, but his ability to bankroll her was another. After their ordeal, she was back to her old ways as if nothing ever happened. Never was that night brought up again. You would think something like this would have changed a person; it did; it made her worse.

PS. SOME PEOPLE ARE USUALLY CHANGED AFTER AN ORDEAL BUT KELIS WAS SO USE TO TGINGS IN HER LIFE GOING AWRY SHE HAD BECOME NUMB TO A LOT OF SHIT. DIFFERENT DAY, SAME SHIT.

CHAPTER 18

STAY IN YOUR LANE

Over time, Darius remained loyal to Kelis and that was something she cherished. Although their relationship was platonic, everyone knew he felt something more. He was willing to give her his heart out of his chest and anything was given and never questioned. As fast as it poured out of her mouth, whatever she wanted was hers. Sasha couldn't understand the connection, because she had no clue how serious Kelis's addiction had gotten. Darius was Kelis's cash cow, and she didn't care who found their relationship weird or felt she had to explain why they were friends. When her addiction had reached its proportion, it was every man onboard. Poor Darius was not the only one fronting her money. Kelis was getting money from a lot of niggas, women husbands and a few bitches that thought she was going to someday, let then lick her pussy. Therefore, there was a time when she felt he owed her something, but after that ordeal in the park, all debts were paid. However, money was something Darius had plenty of and he did not mind sharing.

Furthermore, since Kelis was popular and well-known, hanging out with her made him feel accepted and popular as well. He was like a stray puppy, so cute, and he allowed her to lead him anywhere by the nose. Also, hanging with Kelis, all the pretty girls in the neighborhood suddenly found him interesting. Do you know that old saying that a woman only considers any man attractive until he is in the arms of another woman? Darius was also a gambler, a habit she introduced him to. Being so controlling, he was not allowed to gamble unless in her presence. To keep that from happening, he was not even allowed to show up anywhere without her. Months later, Darius showed up at the spot with two bitches on his arm. He was feeling himself and although he should. Kelis's hypnosis had lost its magic, since he realized he can give some women less and get more. Eventually Darius started coming out without Kelis. How long did she think she was going to be able to keep a man at bay and not give him anything to be loyal for.? Don't ever believe a woman, who tells you, she has a friend, and he supplies all her financial needs, and she don't ever have to fuck him. Maybe not always but you have to feed a hungry dog sometimes, if not he will find somewhere else to eat!

So, this particular night, Darius played poker with some bigtime players and cheaters. He was accustomed to playing the game, but he was inexperienced to play with these cats. Poker is a game of knowing how to stay calm and Darius was not the one for that, especially if there are pretty girls in the room. Part of why Kelis kept a tight hold on him was because he was stupid and naïve, and she wanted to protect him. Darius did not have a chance against these guys and those many shots of tequila made their attempt easier. He was a hustler's dream, and by night's end, he was throwing up all over the place and had lost 10 thousand dollars. Money like that means nothing for a rich boy like Darius, but his money was given in an allotment. His next allowance wasn't due for months and his father had already warned him about spending his money carefully. Normally, Kelis has no remorse or sympathy for anyone who does the crime but can't do the time. Losing is the biggest part of gambling; and she had lost more than her share, and nobody ever put their arms around her or paid her debt. However, Darius was taken advantage of and that was downright unacceptable.

He was introduced to the crew by her, so she felt responsible and also violated. Those guys knew he sponsored her, and those bitch ass mother fuckers were jealous. Yes, some men are just as jealous of a woman, like some women are. Since Darius had always looked out for her, she decided to lend him the money. She gave them two months to pay her back, and if not, Darius would have two problems: her and his daddy. As much as Kelis would love to have taught him a lesson, she wanted to break free of him. He was a good kid, stupid, but he no longer deserved her abuse anymore.

Two months had passed, and Darius had just disappeared. She knew where he lived but did not want to darken his doorstep unless she had to. This matter was nobody else's business, and she really didn't want to involve his parents. After multiple calls and texts... Kelis was forced to go to his house. So, one early Sunday morning, she arrived at his doorstep and was greeted by a woman in curlers and a beaten robe. She was still in yesterday's makeup. She had wondered if this is how the rich go to bed or have, she not. Before Kelis could introduce herself, his mother already knew who she was. Kelis was a celebrity at their house and his mother responded like a groupie. Darius had spoken about her often and they believed his many disappearances were with her.

After a 10-minute introduction, his mother finally informed Kelis that Darius was not home. Kelis knew his mother was lying but left without making any noise. Darius's mother is not the first nor last mother to cover for their child. Too bad his mother had to lie because the next time Kelis has to come back, she will be bringing the truth. Poor Darius, he was out of his league by fucking with Kelis and now she had no choice but to take this matter to another level. Lord knows she did not want to, but it was time that his daddy gets an earful of his son's latest activities. The only thing that had Kelis holding her breath was the fact that Darius's father is very prejudiced about his son's antics. He believes boys will be boys and that male chauvinist attitude is why his son does what he does!

After many nights camped out by Darius's house, Kelis had to go about looking for his father another way. Finally, one day, she lucked up and caught him at one of his construction sites. He owns many sites throughout the city but many of the locations were undisclosed. Kelis knew some people who worked at the DMV that skimmed his license plates from a parked company van in his driveway.

So, one early Tuesday morning, at about 6 am, Kelis showed up at Darius's father's job. She had actually been there since 5 am, staking out her surroundings. When she finally knocked on the trailer door, no other but Mr. Darius Sr. answered. He automatically knew who she was and seemed to be quite smitten with her. Her reasoning for showing up at his job did not raise a red flag and that was weird. He actually never questioned it and was more interested in getting to know her personally. Mr. Darius was just like Kelis imagined. Somehow, throughout his performance, she was able to shove her reasons for being there down his throat. Once she explained her notions, he still was unaffected and continued to go about flirting with her righteously. Mr. Darius' hands were quick, and his mouth was disgusting, but Kelis was used to perverted men. He was just another dog in need of neutering. After the fake preliminaries, he handed Kelis an envelope filled with nothing but hundred-dollar bills. The money was ready for the taken and the well-sort-out game was orchestrated by no other than he and his miserable ass son.

Mr. Darius was well aware that she would be showing up, and for the first time, Kelis was played. Since her high school days, his father has put his son on the front line to get her attention. It all goes back to their high school years when he used to watch her as she would step out of the Limo in the morning to allow his son to get in. Was it the way she got out or the way she slithered in? So, in order for this mission to be accomplished, Darius played stupid, timid, and frightened of his own shadow. What man uses his son to get pussy from a young woman he is currently friends with... a perverted dad?

The cat and mouse game were brilliantly played, but Kelis will get the last laugh. In all means to get even, it was time for Papa Bear to get his, while Baby Bear observes. Kelis and Mr. Darius's relationship was crazy as shit. She never allowed him to fuck her, but he ate the hell out of her pussy daily. Plenty of money was being spent, so in order to keep the gravy train rolling, she knew it was time to give him some pussy. After a while, the long Vegas weekend trips and the elaborate shopping sprees were not enough. She became digestively turned off and would charge him every time, they fucked. Eventually, his heart began to outweigh his bank account, and that is when he decided to leave his family. Their late-night hookups and last-minute weekend trips to Vegas from Fridays to Sunday, were not enough for the old boy. He became so obsessed and demanding and lost all feelings and respect for his wife. Although he continued to pay the mortgage on their home, other bills were no longer being taken care of.

The aftermath of financially taking care of two women regularly put him on the brink of bankruptcy. The second mortgage on his home had him in a bigger chokehold than the one Kelis had on him. Trying so desperately to keep Kelis in his life, he was willing to lose his home and everyone in it. Kelis found his attitude and behavior disturbing and so unattractive. Their time together had run its course because her job here was done! She considered their relationship based on a Poker game and it was time to fold and walk away! After multiple attempts to end their affair, he threatened suicide. Just the mere mention of the word does something to Kelis's spirit, considering her father once killed himself. For a while, Mr. Darius manipulated her with threats, but after a while, she was not going to be emotionally captive. After he realized Kelis was willing to walk away from him, not knowing if he would or would not kill himself, he eventually went back home to his wife. Hopefully, with prayer, his marriage will be able to recover.

Not so long ago, Kelis ran into the whole gang at a car dealership. She was with another gentleman purchasing her an Audi convertible while they were there to buy a family car... an SUV; how boring. By the looks of things, everyone seemed happy. Kelis gestured hello with a gentle wave, but no response was returned. Obviously, there's still some animosity, and Kelis was well aware of why. Hopefully, someday, they would all realize that they all were saved. For the rest of her life, Kelis never forgot how Darius saved her from being raped in the park and him from the streets.

PS. THE STREETS ARE BRUTUAL AND THAT IS WHY SIDEWALKS WERE MADE. SO, IT WAS A WIN WIN FOR VERYONE.

CHAPTER 19

SUKI KIDS RETURN

Several years ago, Suki agreed to be a sperm donor so that his favorite cousin Alexandria and her husband could have children. One day relaxing at home, soaking his feet, sipping Merlo, his doorbell rang! There, through his peephole, was a Caucasian woman in tow with two children. Unaware of who she was, he immediately opened the door. She was a well-dressed perfectly spoken woman. As she entered with the two children, she quickly started her business. She said she was Beatrice Nobles from Child Welfare. Before she could go any further, she asked if he was Shawn Bolden. In a very sassy tone, Suki replied, "Who wants to know?" Ms. Nobles took no time to address her concerns and took no liking to his sassiness. Once Suki realized that Ms. Nobles was there for serious business, he straightened his tone of voice. Before they both got deeper into the conversation, Ms. Nobles asked if the children could be placed in another room. Once they were out of earshot, Suki confirmed his identity.

Ms. Nobles informed Suki that his cousin Alexandria Coleman's children were taken from the home of Samantha Mitchel. Samantha was a current friend of Alexandria. Normally, placement for the children is handled differently, but Ms. Alexandria left specific details that if she did not return, the children should be taken to their biological father... Shawn Bolden. Suki then immediately addressed the matter by saying that the children were fathered through vitro fertilization. How they were created was no concern to Ms. Nobles. Her only concerns were who and how they were going to be placed. Suki then asked if Alexandria's whereabouts were known. Ms. Nobles could not give out such information at the time because the bureau also was unaware of where she was. Suki was now a ball of nerves and nervously tried to explain to Ms. Nobles that he only agreed to be a sperm donor to help his cousin. Ms. Nobles appeared sympathetic, but I am sure she has heard and seen it all. Not knowing what to say or how to deal with this shit, Suki gathered his compulsions and told Ms. Nobles that, unfortunately, he would not be able to take the children. Ms. Nobles kindly said she understood and asked for the children to be let out of the room so that they could go about their business. As she gathered the children and headed towards the door, she said a profound thing… "Sometimes in life, we do not sign up for certain things; some things are destined to happen." Also, if he or any other family members have a change of heart, where she could be reached, and if not, the children would be placed in the foster system.

The idea of the children in the system sickened Suki, but he was adamant about his decision and allowed them to leave with Ms. Nobles. Throughout the confusion, Suki only noticed a little about the children when they were about to leave. The boy had curly hair as he did as a child, and the girl had sunken dimples like his mother. The resemblances of the kids were spell bounding and for days, he could not see anything but their faces. The mere thought of them fluttered his heart, and the thought of them being in foster care made his heart flutter more.

As the days went on, he knew something had to be done and locating Alexandria was part of the puzzle. Obviously, she was once again on a mission and knowing what he knew of her past, there's no telling where she could be. Long ago, street corners and crack houses were plentiful.

Nowadays, the most beautiful houses and neighborhoods secretly harbor them. It was like finding a needle in a haystack and since much of her stomping grounds had changed, that meant he had to start from scratch. First on his agenda was going to question family members. Going to question family was like going to the welfare… you go to get help, but there are so many people in your business. Most of them he had not seen since he was a kid, so this was going to be very interesting.

After that road went south, he had one ace up his sleeve. He was going to find Samantha. Samantha and Alexandria were partners in crime while on the streets. They were known to set up men by drugging and robbing them and it is a wonder neither of them was ever killed. Finding where Samantha lived was not an easy task since she lived like a gypsy. After many knocks on some unpleasant doors and going to many seedy places, Samantha's whereabouts were found. There's a code in the street, and nobody gives up any info about you, but there is always one desperate ass nigga that would sell your soul for a dollar.

Once Suki found out where Samantha was residing, he took along the "GOOD OLD BOYS." Thank goodness he did; that side of town was very dangerous and after many knocks on doors, finally someone answered. The house was indeed a trap house, and rolling with the "GOOD OLD BOYS," you were as safe as if you brought the police along. When the door opened, all six of them went in without an invitation. Once inside, the house was dimly lit, smelly and filthy. There were various dope and cracked heads roaming about, and in the corner of the room, standing looking like a bewildered animal, was Samantha. By looking at Samantha, she was now using heroin. She was feeling good and did not know they had entered the room. Nothing about Samantha had changed much but the black eye she was sporting. Samantha's addiction was in charge, but underneath, you could still see a pretty girl. The "GOOD OLD BOYS" moved around the house to make sure shit was safe. It was like The Walking Dead; everyone was walking around like zombies with battered spirits.

Once Suki got closer up on her, between nods she appeared embarrassed but recognized him. Her would-be boyfriend, aka pimp, was just ass fucked up but tried to get gangster but was thrown on the couch. I bet that woke a mother fucker up! Suki was well known from many corners and had some would-be fans at the house. While patiently waiting for Samantha to get herself together, he struck up various conversations with many of them. Suki was a people person and would talk to almost anybody and loved an audience. Many of them did not know much about one another since the house was used for getting high, not to get acquainted.

One of the male house guests acted as if he knew Alexandria, but that was just a ploy for funds. Suki was willing to pay for information and many tried to make up shit just to get paid. Reportedly this particular crackhead tried to proposition Suki to get a blow job for 10 dollars. First of all, Suki was too fabulous to get his dick sucked by some nasty crackhead. Secondly, blow jobs are his specialty, and he gives them and doesn't care about receiving them. It turns out that one of the "GOOD OLD BOYS" was bisexual and emptied his sac down the homeboy's throat and did not give him a brown penny. They then took Samantha out of the house, and she was literally kidnapped. She was taken back to Suki's apartment, where she could dry out and maybe could be of some help. Being a neat freak and having OCD, bringing her to his pad was a desperate move. He needed to know more about Alexandria and her whereabouts.

After 2 days of detoxing, Samantha told Suki the entire story. Malcolm, her husband, had knee surgery about two years ago. The pain was so unbearable that he was prescribed oxycontin. He was very well aware of the repercussions but could not manage without the medication. Painkillers are so highly addictive. When his doctors were no longer allowed to prescribe him any more pills, he was already addicted. Since heroin was cheaper to afford, that once again became his best friend. That is how he was led back down that road. Alexandria struggled with his relapse. To cope with it, she started sipping wine to relieve some stress. For a while, it did not appear to be a problem, but one wrong move on her part and she was now back indulging as well. Malcolm alone was disgusted by his situation. Once he found out she too was using drugs again, he left, and the rest is history. On several occasions, the children were left with Samantha, but Alexandria would always come back to retrieve them. It was so unsettling to hear what had happened to his cousin and her husband, but the biggest disappointment was what was about to happen to the kids.

When Suki finally got all the information he needed, Samantha was allowed to leave, but she did not want to. After two days of detoxing, shitting, and throwing up all over the place, something spiritual was awakening in her, and she was feeling it. She begged Suki to let her stay for a while and he agreed only if she was really serious about getting clean. After two weeks had passed, Suki went with Samantha to a rehab facility. As she walked solely through those doors, so determined to save her life, she prompted him to do the same for his. Before making anything official, Suki walked the floors many nights. He went into seclusion, and that alarmed Kelis and Blaze. So worried about him, Blaze reached out to Kelis, but she assured him that he needed this time and space. It was such a beautiful thing to see a man be so supportive. It took a while for Kelis to admit, but she was happy that Suki had someone who truly loved and adored him. It was a long time coming, but a change has come!

This decision was not as mathematical as many would love to believe… wanting to be a father is not always the question; knowing if you are capable of being one is the final jeopardy question! Since there were no right or wrong answers, the only thing Suki was left to do was go downtown to that child welfare and get his damn kids. The night prior, he was anxious but yet excited. He was like a new expectant father, nervously pacing in the waiting room, waiting on the arrival of his first newborn. He had plenty of questions, but his main concerns were mostly not how well he would adjust to the kids but how well they would adjust to him. The only answer Kelis ever solicited was that if he followed his heart, GOD would direct him! The conversation left Kelis flabbergasted because who would have ever believed, out of the three of them, Suki would be the first one raising kids? Life is so unpredictable, and no matter how much you plan, God has plans of His own!

Before the sun rose, Suki was fully dressed and made his way downtown. He arrived really early and patiently sat across the street from the building, drinking more coffee than he should. Once the doors finally opened, people appeared out of nowhere and hauled in. Once he got inside, he was quickly seen by Ms. Nobles. After many papers and questions were rendered, he was told to wait in another room. While waiting, all sorts of things ran through his mind. Suddenly he became frighten and the room got really small, and it seemed like all the oxygen had vanished. He was indeed having a panic attack, but when the kids were ushered into the room, a burst of fresh air filled his lungs. The smaller room became a mountain top, and he was standing on top of it with nothing but the sun and sky existing. Suki knew he had to pull it together, if not for himself but for the children.

The first two weeks were incredibly challenging for them all. Personalities were entwined and likes and dislikes were commented on. There were adjustments to be made and being able to adjust to them was the hardest. Suki has always done things his way, from the way he lived his life and how he dismissed those who did not approve! His home was his sanctuary and now it has to be shared with not one child but two. His décor was designed with him in mind and not designed child friendly. Sensual portraits were taken down, while white plush carpeting was taken up. Suki was unquestionably unselfish about parting with a lot of things, but when he was told to tone down his style of dressing, that is where he drew the line. No makeup, stilettos, or bowers will never be boxed away, and he was not playing. He was always known for his fashion sense and without it, he could not exist. It was who he was, and somehow, the children will have to understand. He stands corrected and what does his style of dressing have to do with his parenting skills? He had a way with clothes, like Picasso had with a paintbrush. The ultimate adjustment was having Blaze move out temporarily. That arrangement had him hyperventilating, but he would rather live without Blaze than be caught wearing blue dockers and a pair of loafers. The children's names were Jade and Jada. The boy was five years old and had autism and the girl was almost four. Jade was highly functional, but if not for his speech impairment, he would appear quite normal.

Now that Jada is a grown woman in Buster Browns. She was four, going on 40, and was able to dress and neatly comb her hair. She could hold a grownup conversation with any adult. She talked as if she had been here before, and at some point, you may have to tell her to shut the hell up! Her attentiveness to her brother was loving, but those attributes must have escalated because of his lack of understanding.

One night Suki was awakened by something he smelled burning. He anxiously ran through the apartment to capture the children but was stomped to find Jada frying her brother an egg sandwich. It was such an incredible thing to witness, so he allowed her to continue. As he stood there astonished, he noticed that she could handle a hot frying pan better than the average professional cook. This child knew her way around the kitchen, probably because of many days of being hungry. Regardless of how she learned, knowledge is power and when you're desperate enough, you would do whatever it takes to suffice. Suki's little girl came well assembled, with grown woman abilities, but she was only four yrs. old. No matter how grown she may be, Suki is going to make sure she enjoys being a child. Furthermore, when the time comes, she'll have not on her father to teach her but two loving aunts… Sasha and Kelis.

CRAZY THING… BY DECIDING TO TAKE FULL RESPONSIBILITY FOR HIS CHILDREN, PROBABLY GAVE THEM A GREATER CHANCE AT A BETTER LIFE. BUT UNEXPECTIVELY WHEN THEY ENTERED, THEY BROUGHT MORE MEANING AND REASONSONING TO HIS.

CHAPTER 20

ENDING OF A RELATIONSHIP

Lately, Kelis has been the overseer of everyone's being and somehow has been neglecting herself. She and Sasha's friendship had flat line, for a minute after Kelis had accepted the offer to be Godmother to Suki's kids. In time, after careful analysis, Sasha seems to be no longer bitter about how things occurred and has casually mentioned that maybe someday she could meet his kids. Accepting the offer to be the Godmother was like accepting the job to be President of the United States! Oh, what a privilege, but too much damn work! Taking on such a role will have its stipulations because if Suki thinks that Kelis is going to be giving up her weekends while he is out painting the town, he better hang a sign in the window that reads... GOD MOTHER WANTED! If so, she would not be the best candidate for this job.

Her freedom meant everything to her and even gave up a good man because of it. Although staying home many nights with children is a whole lot better than staying home with a man that acts like one. Speaking of Bleu has been trying to catch up with Kelis for weeks and she has been hiding and avoiding him at all costs. She was aware that, eventually, they'd cross paths, but once they did, she knew she would have to explain to him about her whereabouts. That was the bullshit she didn't feel she needed to do. She was a grown woman, and the last person she felt entitled to lie about her comings and goings was her grandmother. Therefore, a must-have conversation was way overdue, and she had made up her mind that it was going to take place this morning.

Bleu lived all the way up in Yonkers and the flow of this morning's traffic was good. Just when you are not in a hurry to be someplace, all things work in your favor. As much as Kelis needed to have this conversation with Bleu, there's a part of her that wishes she did not! What she needed to say was well rehearsed and memorized, and still, she is somewhat indecisive. The realization is she and Bleu had a good run, but the constant bumping of heads left bruises and a bitch dizzy. To make matters more confusing, their sex life was on fire, but it was when they got out of bed things took a nasty turn. If only they could have spent their whole life in bed fucking and don't think they didn't try. Sometimes, two people on different paths can find their way back to one another, but not when one is driving a car, and the other is boarding a plane. Having different views, likes and dislikes is healthy, but controlling issues will never work, unless the other person doesn't mind being controlled. Bleu wants to believe that all a woman wants is to be married. Getting married is something most women do want but not if her soon to be husband has old-fashioned values.

Kelis was just 25 years old and watched her grandmother get married young and have a house full of babies. Although her grandmother never spoke of being unhappy, I am sure she had days where she wished she could walk away and do it all over again. Furthermore, Kelis believed Bleu wouldn't be the last to offer that life, and since she thought the world owed her something, next! Her beauty allowed her to think the way she did and get away with shit the average woman couldn't. Not only was she beautiful, but she was intelligent enough to know that someday, her beauty would be invaluable to any prospective buyers! She believed that she and Bleu had a good thing going and without the pressures of committing and with a little space in between, who knows what would become of them. Why would he want to spoil things with matching rings and babies? This was Kelis's first breakup, and she took it like a champ. There would be no going to bed crying, just a box of chocolates or another mother fucker.

Nevertheless, Kelis has lost so much in her life, and her abandonment issues seem to heighten every time a love is lost. Finally, she arrived at Bleu's crib, and for privacy reasons, she alerted him by calling his phone but got no answer. Thank goodness, a spare key was kept under the mat because it had started raining heavily outside. As she slowly turned the lock, a second lock intervened. It was totally surprising because never is the second lock ever used, unless Bleu is out of town or during the night. Suddenly, she was not able to turn the lock because, obviously, Bleu was on the inside, turning it also.

When the door opened, he was wearing nothing but sweat with a gun in his hand. The look on his face was priceless, but the bitch standing behind him had the money shot. For a minute, everything was in slow motion and then everything froze. The girl ran into the room, and Bleu started to run after her, but Kelis dared him to make a move. Kelis then slowly moved past him and closed the door.

Once inside the apartment, Kelis made herself at home. She went to the bar, made herself a drink, and offered one to them both. Once her drink was made, she walked into his bedroom, where the poor girl was getting dressed. The girl was cute, light-skinned with a well-paid-for body. Kelis was a little surprised that Bleu went for that type, considering he had always admired her chocolate complexion and natural body. At that moment, Bleu had put some pants on and demanded that Kelis not start anything with the girl.

"What do you think I am, some fucking animal," she replied? Unexpectedly, Kelis and the girl went about things like grownups. During their conversation, Kelis removed all her clothes and stripped them down to nothing. Bleu could not believe where she was going with that, but just like most men, I bet he thought he was about to get treated with a threesome. While the conversation went into high gear, Kelis decided a blunt would be necessary and also some champagne.

Before you know it, they all got comfortable and got fucked up. Just when the last blunt was smoked and three bottles of champagne were emptied, Kelis walked up to the girl and started touching her softly as Bleu watched. While Kelis was touching his girlfriend, Bleu used his familiar hands-on Kelis. Before you knew it, they all were naked and touching one another. Slowly, Kelis took Bleu to his bed and laid him down. Suddenly, his bitch was feeling the vibe and tried to take control, but Kelis showed her who she was and always will be. Kelis then climbed into bed with Bleu and fucked him right in front of his girlfriend.

In the beginning, he reached for her, but once he and Kelis got started, he forgot she was there. The pathetic girl stood over them, waiting for her turn, but never did she get a chance to join them. What she did not know was Kelis wasn't into chicks but big dicks and that was Bleu's. After it was all over, Kelis got dressed and before she walked out the door, she rolled another blunt for the road and bid goodbye. Leaving his apartment, she was a slightly scorn woman because had she not been, she would've never done that girl the way she just did. That girl did nothing to her, but yet she was in the crossfire. Seeing Bleu with another woman was bound to   happen; she just wished it would happen in a different place and time. The only thing she regretted about that day was that she allowed a man to embarrass a woman. Soon after that time, she and Bleu decided to remain friends. During their last conversation, not too much was spoken about his girl, but Kelis believes he blew it. Not too many women can watch their man get fuck by another woman. and because of that, is the reason she does not understand having a threesome with someone you love.

The ride home was slow, and the radio played every slow jam ever made. Kelis was a hard nut to crack, but the right song and temperament can make anyone feel melancholy.

PS. SUPRISINGLY, A FEW TEARS DID FELL BUT MAINLY FOR THE MANY LOVED ONES SHE HAS LOST.

CHAPTER 21

GOLDEN GIRLS REUNION

Finally, everything she had gone through with Bleu was behind her, but she was desperate for a hug and words of encouragement from her two best friends. Long-lived the days when you saw one, you saw the other. Since Suki and she have been communicating more these days, her best bet was to go to his home. Brooklyn Heights is such a beautiful neighborhood, with many aligned brownstones in a row. Many people bought these million-dollar houses but don't have anywhere to park their cars. She arrived at his apartment unannounced, and his neighbor informed her that he had just left to get the children from school. Thank goodness the rain had stopped, and the sun was shining bright; she was able to sit on his stoop until he returned. A no soliciting sign hung on the gate, but like elsewhere, she follows her own rules.

While sitting on his steps, memories of growing up in Brooklyn came to her. The building was definitely different, but the steps were almost a replica. The children's school was not too far from his apartment, so she couldn't imagine what was taking him so long to return. Just when she got up to stretch her legs, she looked up the block and noticed Suki and his children walking with another woman. As the group got closer, the height, walk, and attire of the person became very recognizable. Could it be? Yes, it was Sasha! When the children finally noticed Kelis on the steps, they started sprinting, but it was Kelis doing most of the running. She was happy to see them but happier to see Sasha with them. They all rejoiced in the middle of the block and made so much commotion that someone thought the cops needed to be called. They were all hollering and screaming so loud that people on the block came out of their homes, thinking someone was hurt. The children were not aware of their past troubles, so all the noise they were making was coming from extremely happy kids. Once inside the apartment, the excitement grew. This was the kind of reception a girl needed and thoughts of any of her problems vanished.

As the day started dwindling down, Suki went into Mommie mode. It was a beautiful thing to see how well he took care of his children. After homework was done and baths taken; it was Nite Nite. Nighttime was the right time because now adults can be adults. No more watching what you say, and you can drink your shit right out of the bottle if you want to. Suki once had a mini wine fridge that is now filled with apple juice boxes and milk. No fret, he has one in the closet of his bedroom, filled with the most expensive bottles of champagne and wine, and if you go to Sasha's condo, you will find it is not as packed as it once was... LOL! They had everything necessary to get this party started: good music, drinks, weed, and straight talk.

After two bottles down, the girls switched to their favorite Cognac and that is when the party took wings. Not only was Hennessey a good drink, but it was also a truth serum. They were friends that had moved on from some serious deep shit, but there was still lots to be said. Before the conversation started, they all agreed to state any issues they had or forever hold their peace. Therefore, after today, all is forgotten and forgiving. The first to get on their soapbox was Suki (of course). He did not go into many details but did admit he was happier than he had ever been. You can tell he wanted to go into details about his life with Blaze but didn't know how it would affect Sasha. Tonight was about being truthful and no holds barred, and if they were going to move on from this, there had to be no holding back.

Nevertheless, Sasha told Suki that she was freed from that part of her life. Once, she confirmed her happiness, he couldn't shut his mouth. He went on and on about himself, Blaze and the children, while all Sasha and Kelis could do was laugh. Thank goodness, Sasha was able to forgive him because although Suki was going to continue to live his life, her forgiveness made it all worthwhile. Maybe this may be prematurely speaking but maybe someday they all can be in the same space without feeling any animosity. As the night continued, more tears flowed. Why is it that whenever girlfriends get together and plenty of drinks are poured, tears are always on the horizon?

Next on the podium was Sasha, and oh boy, did she preach. Before she got started, she cussed Suki the fuck out but with love. She then said that had Blaze not been the love of his life, she would have never forgiven him. She indeed took some of the blame by saying keeping her relationship private was not a good idea. Private affairs are only befitting for a cheating man. If any man wants to keep your relationship private, he has the opportunity to fuck, you, your sister, and your mother and none of you would know. She then admitted what role her parents played in the matter and when addressing her parents, Suki and Kelis put their drinks down and sat up at attention. She said that over the years, her parents' controlling and negative attitude towards people started to weigh heavily on her. As much as they both wanted to agree out loud, they knew talking negatively about anyone's parents or children was highly nonnegotiable.

She also said that the minute Blaze entered her life, they tried to do everything they could to break them up. Blaze was good enough to attend her father's entrepreneur program but was not good enough for his daughter. No matter how much he succeeded and did well, he was always looked on as the help. To them, he was never going to measure up to being anything but an educated hood rat. Placing many young men in his mentoring program was only designed to make him look good and richer. Sadly, her father had forgotten where he came from and was only concerned about where he was headed. Her mother turned a blind eye to his shit, so that made her just as guilty. She had become very sickened by the kind of people her parents had become. She knew her father was driven by money and enjoyed a certain kind of lifestyle, which they all had grown accustomed to enjoying, but his prejudices were nauseating. So, after contemplating the situation, Sasha went to her parents in hopes of a truce.

That very night, he was more disgusting than ever and had the audacity to bring up Blaze's prison record. Blaze's prison record was public knowledge, and everyone, especially her father, knew of his time spent in prison. At the same time, this was coming from a man who, at one time, went to juvenile prison for bad boys because he and some friends stole a car when he was 14 years old. Although the two crimes can't be compared, who knows where his life would've been had someone given him a second chance. Breaking down Blaze's portfolio was stupidity on his part since he was the one who approved his application. After leaving her father's office in tears, she headed to the condo to pack her bags.

One hour into packing, her parents came after her. Instead of leaving things where they were, her father continued to manipulate and control the situation. There was no way to get him to shut up, so she had to pull out the big guns. At this time, her timid mother was upset and needed to go lie down. *"Yes, Mother, go lay down because you don't need to hear this,"* she said to herself. Then she told him, "How dear you try to play, Mr. Perfect. Don't you know, I am not the one to fuck with? You better leave me alone, or I'll tell your wife about all the women and sometimes men you have been bringing to the condo for years during the day." He tried to deny it, but that is when she took him to the library, slid the bookshelf to the side and revealed the hidden room. She claimed her father's face dropped, but not as much as Suki's and Kelis's when they were told the story. She said she never spoke about his secret because she never wanted to believe it. The next day, a letter was left on the foyer table from her father, saying that …he loved her and only wanted what was best for her. Also, the condo was hers, and anything she ever needed, he would always be there.

After Sasha got through with her truth, Suki got up and said, "Are you telling me, after all those years the way he always judged me, he was also packing fudge?" "Yes, Suki and I will never discuss this again because, right or wrong, he is still my father." After everyone said what was ailing them, it was Kelis's turn. One thing for sure, Kelis was not an emotional creature. The many relationships and traumas she had in her life she dealt with alone and speaking about didn't make it better but sometimes worse, considering who she spoke to. To be a team player, she did mention a little about Bleu and them officially calling it quits. At first, the bureau did not believe her, but then they noticed she was sincere. Suddenly, the room went silent, and just when she was about to speak, she didn't. On her way over, she felt something, but that moment had passed, and now she felt nothing.

Nevertheless, she will place Bleu with all the other men in her life, which is not worth mentioning.

Sasha and Suki knew there was more to the story, and out of respect for each other's feelings, they left her alone with hers. They are all growing up and finally realizing that as much as they love one another, other people will enter their lives, and they would love just as much. So, glasses were raised, and Kelis said,

PS. HERE'S TO GOOD HEALTH, WEALTH AND HAVING 99 PROBLEMS, BUT A MAN WILL NEVER BE ONE.

CHAPTER 22

FINDING KELIS

Last week at Suki's house was very therapeutic and we all established a newfound respect for one another. That day was one of the best and funniest times Kelis had ever spent with her people. There was plenty of grown folk talk and no fakeness. Every so often, amongst real friends, those conversations need to be had. Without proper sunlight and water, a flower will wither away, and so could a friendship without proper justification. The funniest moment was when Sasha and Kelis teased Suki about how he dresses the kids. Luckily, they attend a private school that requires uniforms. Dressing Jada was simple because everything he put her on, he once wore similar or just like. It was refreshing to see that most times, he would put her on beautiful dresses that came to her knees, with some ridiculously cute patent leather Mary Janes. Now, when it came to Jade, that is where shit gets tricky. Suki knew nothing about men's attire except their footwear. Jade had every sneaker there was, but when Suki put him on those satin shorts, there was more laughter than on comedy "Deaf Jam". Jade had already been picked on because of his speech problem and those shiny shorts gave the kids more ammunition. However, Suki relied on designer clothes, and everyone knows that people who hide behind labels have no fashion sense of their own. The children's attire was the least of anyone's worries because they had three people who were going to make sure they pretty much had everything they wanted and needed.

The club was doing much better, mainly because Kelis and Porsche decided that a business manager was needed. Pouring drinks and knowing how to cut a card game does not require many skills, but how the entire sausage is made takes a whole lot of skilling. However, one of the "GOOD OLD BOYS" suggested that he would be good for the job, but Kelis was very reluctant to hire him. He was recently hired for security and had not shown any disloyalty, but he was guilty by association. The "GOOD OLD BOYS" were on their way out and Kelis had no intentions of hiring any of them for anything else. Who knew either of them could spell or count past 10? Visibly, their only skills were tormenting, manipulating, and bullying people. After consulting Big Whiz on the idea, he suggested they hire a familiar person more so than a stranger. Even from the words of Big Whiz, Kelis still felt uncomfortable hiring anyone, but after multiple interviews, a business manager was hired. His name was Zane.

Zane was a nice young man who was given the nickname insane because he made the women crazy. Zane was cute and had brains underneath his muscular physique. He was nothing like those other muscle-bound idiots who could not read past the 5th-grade level and tended to date women also in the 5th grade. Taking advice from anyone has always been Kelis's downfall, but she knew that if so, Big Whiz was the only one she would consider since her grandmother trusted him with her. He became her only confidante, and when she allowed herself to pay attention, he taught her some very important things.

However, Big Whiz was of a certain age now and he and the streets had parted ways many years ago. Although most of the things he taught Kelis would carry her a long way, the streets are now nothing like when he ruled them. The mafia was known to move the biggest amount of heroin to this country, but now, just about anyone could do it with the right amount of money and connections. Speaking of the mafia, they also are no longer the biggest organized gang; Gangs now originate from various countries, states, cities, and boroughs. Just look around; the mightiest and most powerful gangs are sometimes a group of boys living right on our same block. Therefore, his old-school knowledge was helpful, but she and Porsche still had so much more to worry about.

At the first meeting held, Zane suggested that the club needed a makeover. Visual presentation was everything and the club needed an upscale look in order to attract a certain clientele. The carpet needed to match the drapes, so that meant its interior needed to be as beautiful as its exterior. Everything was multiplied, ranging from the bartenders and the bouncers. Not much had changed as far as the girls were concerned, since many of them were perfectly fine. They were handpicked, pretty, and danced very well. The only problem the club needed was space. The basement measured 1,800 sq ft, with a bar that took up most of the room, four poker tables, a large crap table and a few cocktail tables. Everything had its own space and the pole that was needed for the girls to perform was an extra addition to the room. Talks of relocating were brought up and like then and now the answer is still…no.

Kelis does have dreams of owning her own club one day and even going legit. Going legit is not an easy thing to do, that is why many do not. Requiring a liquor license, along with a whole lot of other things makes the idea more unbelievable. But the constant looking over your shoulders and the late nights make you want to dream on. Kelis was beginning to be sickened not only by what it took to run a club but to those that visited. She had become sick and tired of being sick and tired and so highly addicted to the lifestyle she couldn't stop now. The results led to her being sleep-deprived and not eating well. Kelis was a hustler among a lot of things, but mostly very vain. She took pride in how she looked and knew it was her ace up her sleeve. So, speaking of lack thereof, a much-needed nap was on the horizon, so she took the time to go lay down.

Just when she was about to close her eyes, she noticed she had a missed call from her mom's facility. Normally, calls from the facility send her nerves into orbit, but these days, her mother's tantrums were far in between and less harmful. No matter how comfortable she has gotten over her mother's overall health, all calls are to be taken immediately. While driving across the bridge, she received another call and that is when she really got worried. When she finally pulled into the parking lot of the facility, she noticed two ambulances and many of the staff outside. Ambulances parked outside the sanitarium were the norm, so she did not panic. Once inside, the nurse who normally takes care of her mom was sitting alone with her hands in her face, and still nothing registered. Then, someone out of nowhere offered her their condolences. She looked around to see who they might be talking to and that is when she realized it was her. She then ran five flights up to her mother's room and when she finally got there, her mother was in her bed with the covers over her face. Suddenly, her legs weakened, and she fell to the floor. She tried her best to get up, but her legs wouldn't allow her to. The floor owned her and that is when she began to crawl. In the midst of crawling, she heard her grandmother's voice, reminding her to stay strong. Her grandmother's spirit was indeed in the room and inside of her. Somehow, when she got to her mother's bed, she dug deep and managed to pull herself up along the railings of the bed. Slowly, she pulled the covers from her mother's face. Finally, her mother was at peace, and it was about time. The day had finally arrived, and even though she knew it was going to happen, it did not make it any easier. The anguish was overbearing and finally the only tears she would shed were for her grandmother and mother. As she lay on her chest, in hopes of wanting to hear another heartbeat, someone touched her shoulder. Thinking it was management or the coroners, it was Porsche. The only other human being on this planet that gave a fuck, her mother's sister. As much as Kelis loved her grandmother, the pain of losing her mother was so much different. Her grandmother raised her and loved her dearly, but her mother, her creator, enough said! Losing her father to suicide before she was born and now today her mother, she is officially an orphan.

After she and Porsche had their moment, the coroners came into the room to take the body. They were very sympathetic to her needs and allowed them to spend as much time as they needed. When it was time to leave, she watched them put her mother in the back of the van, she ran screaming for one last look. Understandably, they declined because normally, after the coroner zips up the body in the bag, the next viewing is either to identify or to prepare for their funeral. Her mother's long-time suffering was over, and hopefully, hers was not beginning. She often wondered if her mother had died from a stroke, cancer, or any other accidental occurrence, would losing her be more accepting? The autopsy later revealed that her mother died from deterioration of the brain that stemmed from depression. Over the years, her mental state worsened, and then malnutrition intervened. The brain is a major part of our anatomy because the brain sends signals to the heart, lungs and kidneys.

Too bad Kelis's mother used up all the love she had for her father and left none for herself. The next day was the hardest for Kelis because she wanted to wake up from this nightmare. Once she realized it was not a dream, she once again became embedded in grief. Fortunately, after her mother's death, plenty of memories she never revisited resurfaced.

She started to remember when she was a child, coming into her mother's room at night. She would hop in bed with her so her mother could comb her hair. Kelis's hair was long and thick but cottony soft, compliments to her father.

Also, she remembered when she had first got her menstrual. It was a hot day in June and the temperature that day had soared higher than normal. Kelis was sitting on the stoop, like always and for all days, she had on a pair of white shorts. She suddenly felt moist below but blamed most of it on perspiration. After a while, she began to feel too moist and uncomfortable, so she decided to go into the house to check beneath. As she got up, the few people sitting on the stoop, mostly boys, noticed the stain. Turns out, she had gotten her period. Her grandmother had already told her about this day happening, but it was an embarrassment, especially for the boys. When it happened, there was nobody home at the house, but her mother. Not knowing if her mother could be of any help, she went to her room anyway. She always wanted her mother to be the go-to person in her life when something went wrong, but never could she bank on her state of mind. All Kelis had to do was show her mother the mess and she went right into mommy mode. It was like her illness took a sudden vacation, and, at that moment, she showed her how to clean herself properly and how to use a sanitary pad. Even though Kelis knew the drill, she played dumb and let her mommy be a mommy!

There was one other memorable moment Kelis would never forget. She had a crush on a cute boy that lived on the block and everyone in her family knew, especially her mother. The window to her mother's room had a great view of the stoop where Kelis played as a kid. One day as she sat on her stoop, being a boy, he teased her about her tiny, slanted small eyes. Coming from a boy she liked, that hurt her feelings and after tolerating his obnoxiousness, he put gum in her hair. Putting gum in a girl's hair is like ruing her favorite bag or shoe, it just cannot happen! So furious with his ass, she demanded he leave her steps and when he did not, she chased him down the block. While she was running after him, she fell and bruised her knee. Her knees were bleeding and skinned very badly and that brought her to tears. When she came into the house, her mother automatically gave her knees the first aid treatment. For hours, Kelis cried, and although she wanted her mother to believe it was because of the bruises, her mother secretly knew it was because of the boy. Kelis never revealed the real truth and allowed her mother to believe what she wanted. Nevertheless, those hugs were priceless, and many wounds that day were taken care of.

Today's her mother's cremation, and just like her grandmother's, it would be quick and private. That particular day was very cold, maybe the coldest day ever. The air was brittle, and the wind was howling through the naked tree branches. Lexus was back from Chicago and looking more fabulous than ever. She had no intention of returning to New York so soon, but the death of her sister gave her no other choice. Kelis wished her aunt's return was under better circumstances, but it was still good to have her back home, even for a few days.

After the cremation, there was no restaurant to visit but a nice two-hour gathering of the three at her mother's final resting place. Kelis's mother was laid to rest alongside her grandmother, and the tombstone read: I WILL ALWAYS LOVE YOU, MOMMY! FINALLY, YOU AND DADDY WILL SEE EACH OTHER AGAIN. UNTIL WE MEET AGAIN, I WILL FOREVER HOLD MY BREATH!!!!

A year had passed, and everything was different except the pain of losing her mother. Owning a club was no longer a priority of hers. Being with friends was cool, but everyone was doing their own thing. Basically, they were all growing in different directions. The long hours at the club were tedious, and it seemed like the more hours put in, the harder it was still to make the rent. Most of her money made, Kelis was fucking it up, mostly to feed her gambling addiction. You would think running your own gambling business, you would have unlimited access to funds. But that was sure not the case.

Have you ever heard the saying, do not get high on your own supply? Obviously, that did not apply to Kelis. Gambling was her choice of drug, and it devoured her like cancer. If diagnosed, she would be in stage four. Death and taxes are the sure thing in life, but someone forgot to mention bills. Every so often, people do miss payments on important things but eventually catch up, but when your money is needed for only one particular thing, there are repercussions to pay. Just remember, no one just doesn't pay their rent. All it takes is one month of falling behind and sometimes when you look up, you're either sleeping on someone's sofa or sleeping on the streets. Once upon a time, a packed house at the club meant plenty of money was being made, but these days, Kelis continues to be all about getting paid but wants to do so without the rumbustiousness of others. She was craving the lifestyle more but was willing to do less to maintain it. Her newfound persona was stressing her out, and although she always had a kick-ass personality, she had become nastier. Along with her own problems, her workers were adding more stress to her life. The strippers were demanding more money and started stealing each other's tips. She had a tight security team to watch everything, but obviously, they started watching more ass, than anything else. Heavy on her list of vultures were those fucking crooked cops. They wanted more hush money, more money than she could afford. She was already mishandling the funds and her business manager was getting suspicious. Zane was smarter than she thought, so when he came to her for answers, she had any. He knew something was not right and knew if she didn't turn the books over to him, he would be beating a dead horse. Kelis didn't allow anyone to write her checks in hopes of not getting robbed, but it turns out she was the one that was doing the robbing.

She was frustrated and on the brinks of bankruptcy. Finally, she considered going to Gamblers Anonymous. The thought frightened her mostly because she finally was willing to admit she had a problem. Although she was considering it deep inside; she was still in denial. So instead of going to Rehab, she decided that maybe a nice quaint vacation somewhere would help. Many places came to mind; and thoughts of going to the Maldives, Rio De Janeiro, or even Africa was thought of. Kelis wanted to go far away as possible and maybe not come back. The very next day, she was relaxing in bed contemplating her next move, when Diamond called. He was going out to Vegas on a business trip and wanted her to meet him out there. Talk about the devil being busy!

At first, she did struggle with the idea, but you know, a bitch, rather be sitting around a poker table talking shit than around a group of people talking about theirs. So, the next morning, instead of rehab, she was on the first thing smoking. All she needed was a major credit card, some form of birth control, some cash, and her Bible! She left Brooklyn with nothing but the clothes on her back. She believed in traveling light and the only thing she took was her intentions of breaking through. She thought positively and knew the worst thing that could happen was maybe a bad sunburn or no vacation dick?

Upon leaving, she was glad she and Porsche were in a good place because she did not want to leave with any ill animosity lingering. Therefore, the club was at its worst, and she thought maybe with her gone, it might get better. Although the trip was for a couple of weeks, deep down inside, she knew it might be longer. Not properly saying goodbye to Sasha and Suki was very unsettling, but she was not in the mood for any mushy see you later performances. She vowed to call them when she gets settled and if she decides to never come back, that too she would handle at her timing. Kelis has always been like a mother hen to her friends, and in her absence, she knew they were doing well and would be fine.

Finally, Sasha has found love; his name is Cruising. His government name is Christopher, but only those close to him are allowed to call him by his birth name. He and Sasha met in the lobby of her condo while visiting his family. They have been dating for about a year now and after recent terms of events, she decided to share the news with her best friends. Although he comes off a little thuggish, he is sweet as honey. He, too, came from money, and you wouldn't know it, considering how down-to-earth he is. He invested some of his inheritance in a few businesses throughout Brooklyn and Queens. He has a little boy from a previous relationship and loves kids. Running down this guy's entire resume, comes off a little thirsty but Kelis was so happy for her friend, and would brag about him forever.

The flight to Vegas was leaving from JFK at 9:45 am, and while sitting in the airport, it dawned on her that she had never traveled alone. Deciding to go solo was not a hard choice, but a scary one. Although she will be hooking up with Diamond, they both have different needs and not much time to fulfill them. Leaving friends behind gave packing light a whole new meaning. Traveling with her posse was not only entertaining, but she felt safe. One year, they all went to the Cayman Islands and never left the compound. They stayed at a six-bedroom villa equipped with their own chef, bartender and even someone to roll their blunts. Their many vacations were legendary, and the dreadful hangovers made them all worthwhile. As she sat in the Uber, she looked through the rear-view mirror and promised to never look back on anything ever again. She was in search of something but knew deep down inside she had already found it but was not ready to claim it.

PS… RAISE YOUR GLASSES. THIS IS FOR THOSE WHO CAN AND CANNOT. ADDICTION IS A MOTHER FUCKER AND IT TAKES A BAD MOTHER FUCKER TO BE RID OF IT.

CHAPTER 23

VEGAS

Kelis's plane landed at 3:06 Vegas time. The weather was typical for that time of year… dry but very warm! The flight was filled with a lot of turbulence, befitting her mood. She decided if she was going to go to Vegas, she was going to do it in grand style. Therefore, a first-class ticket was purchased at the airport and a luxurious suite at the Bellagio Hotel was booked for an endless stay. The room amenities included a fully stocked wet bar, a private masseuse, and an around-the-clock room service. You could probably fit 25 people comfortably in the bathroom and at least 10 in the shower. The shower had powerful multiple shower heads that forcefully streamed water in every direction. The water vigorously claimed parts of her body, she forgot existed. The most important thing about this whole damn experience, she made it happen for herself! A trip like this is usually sponsored by some dude hoping to get seriously laid, but this time around, there will be no faking any headaches or orgasms. This was her time, to prevail and if all fails, she will get up and start all over again!

On her first day in Vegas, she wanted to just settle in and do a little shopping. The warm weather made shopping easy and all she would need at the moment was a couple of pairs of shorts and some tank tops. The humidity had a girl's face glistering, but her hair wasn't feeling it at all. She had what they called good hair. What in the hell is good hair? The best texture of hair is full, not brittle, and could sustain anything you do to it. Kelis knew her hair was different from many women of her culture but never could understand what was so good about it. The only two things she did know about her hair where it did not require a perm, and after seven days unwashed, it smelled sour.

When checking in, she noticed a lot of cute guys checking in as well. She questioned the number of men in the hotel and thought maybe they were there for a convention or some massive bachelor party. Therefore, their sexualities were questioned since men do not vacation together. Nevertheless, many of them were very young and young men have never been Kelis's cup of tea, but you know what they say… but you know what's done in Vegas stays in Vegas! So hopefully a do not disturb sign will be forever hung on her room. Her hotel suite was fabulous, and she took much pleasure enjoying her enormous waterfall of a shower. Suddenly when she and her shower head were getting acquainted, she was interrupted by a thunderous knock on the door.

The loud pounding on the door sounded like the police, and for a moment, her first reaction was to flush something. Suddenly, she was reminded of her surroundings and immediately jumped out of the shower. Without hesitation or a robe, she aggressively flung the door open, wearing nothing but a belly chain. Standing at the door were seven concierges with many bundles of flowers. They were completely lost for words and had more water coming out of their mouths than she had coming off her body. As they moved into the room slowly and nervously, she directed them where to place the flowers. When leaving, they exited quickly, but one asshole dragged his foot. They were not giving a tip because they had received something more valuable than money. The viewing of the best piece of ass they will ever lay their eyes on. The room was filled with black orchids, her favorite flower. Some say they symbolize death, but their rarity and exoticness were the reasons she thought they were so beautiful. Orchids, being her favorite flower, were a secret that not too many people knew about. She could count on one hand who knew and on that very small list of people, was Bleu. So confident that he was the culprit, she never bothered to read the card. Somehow, her whereabouts were no longer her secret, and on that very short list of big mouths, was Suki. Sending flowers to her hideout was cool, but trying to show up unannounced was not. There was a time when Kelis would do just about anything to hide things from Bleu, but this is a different ballgame. If he comes to the park to play, he better bring a bigger bat to the plate. Later, it acknowledged that at least 300 orchids were delivered at 40 dollars per flower. It didn't take Einstein to calculate the math and Stevie Wonder to see the bullshit. A room filled with beautiful flowers does not work anymore for Kelis, even her precious orchids. A man has to bring more to the table than something she already possessed. Take note, ladies, you are the flower and don't get caught up in the bouquets given to you.

Furthermore, Bleu and many hustling niggas like him make fast money and spend it very quickly. When it's easily made, it's easy come and easy go and eventually, so do you! Her unexpected assignment for today was to get concierges to send the flowers to the nearest funeral parlor or, better yet, hand them out to any woman who came into the hotel. The afternoon went long and after multiple calls to management, nobody still came to retrieve the flower. The situation was about to get her stressed, so she went about her business. She had bigger fish to fry and an afternoon date with her shower head. It had three speeds, which she loved but desired one! Kelis preferred the fast and vigorous speed but would take the old-fashioned route any day. This little gem of a secret is known to many old heads, but it is time to school the young queens. First, turn on the water and select a temperature that agrees with you. Slide up towards the faucet with your legs wide open. Make sure the water is turned on at its highest. Then, take a washcloth and fold it in half. Place that cloth across the water facet. Slide up closely to the faucet while aiming the water directly at your clit… Baby, it's the best orgasm a woman can have besides when she uses her own fingers. Queens don't be embarrassed; masturbation is the safest, accountable lover a girl could ever have. He does not cheat on her; he is always pleasurable, and she is aware of his whereabouts at all times.

After she had finished pleasuring herself, it was time to hit the streets. She then quickly tied her hair up and slipped on the shortest pair of shorts she owned. This was her first night in Vegas and she was determined to enjoy herself by just observing the atmosphere. Her walk through the casino was like it was everywhere, all eyes on her. The streets of Brooklyn were unlike Vegas, but the same walk applied. As she sashayed through the casino, men everywhere stopped what they were doing. She had an audience and was putting on the ultimate show when suddenly someone grabbed her from behind. Their hands were placed over her eyes, but the smell of their cologne was so familiar. Vegas was known to have some of the craziest, creepiest people, but if this was some weirdo, oh boy, did they smell damn good.

The only man that smelled that damn delicious was Bleu and Diamond. As she turned around, she had all bets on Diamond being the one covering her eyes. Yes, it was him, smelling good and looking like a million bucks.

Her love for Diamond was real and they were known as the "Will and Grace" of the neighborhood. She was ecstatic to see him, and her face glowed. There was so much to talk about with not much time to do so. It's been a minute since Diamond and Kelis had seen one another and since that day at the Marriot Hotel, their conversations have been short and far between. She was happy to be with someone she knew amongst a sea of strangers. But that was just too bad because it was too late to be scared or homesick. After their brief encounter, they both parted ways since they were on entirely different missions.

She was on to do some shopping while he was on to do what the fuck Diamond does best... Shopping in Vegas was almost like shopping anywhere else. The clothes were a bit more fashionable but more expensive. Kelis was no stranger to fashion but was unfamiliar with buying her own clothes. From the time she was a child, her clothes were sorted by the best boosters in NY or many shopping sprees sponsored by other men. After spending nearly 10 thousand dollars, she was pissed, but not necessarily because of the money she spent, but the bags were light. The bags contained a sexy black dress, two pairs of shoes, two pocketbooks, along with a few pairs of thongs, some toiletries, and one good pushup bra. Besides the Gucci clutch, everything else was mediocre shit bought from a boutique. Everyone knows boutiques can be very pricey. Maybe because their merchandise is unique, and they often never have more than two of anything. Therefore, when a bitch is seen in public with something fly, chances are, she would not be a duplicate of the next woman's getup. An afternoon of shopping wiped Kelis out, mainly because of the hot desert heat and hours of walking around.

It was time to make some calls and hopefully get some rest for her big night ahead. Napping during the day, especially in Vegas, is not something most people do, unless they have been up the entire night. The only thing that could probably put Kelis to sleep during those hours is a good fuck and that still determined, who she fucked? These days, Kelis remains tired and mostly because, she is mentally frustrated. Before her head hit the pillow, she noticed a few missed calls. She had left her phone in her room and wasn't aware of them. The calls were from back home and addressed. Everything and everybody were OK and knowing that gave her an all of a sudden burst of energy that had her blood pumping. It finally dawned on her that she was in Vegas, and she had not come here to sleep.

In one hour, she was showered and dressed. It took her no time to slide into some very short shorts, a tank top, and flip-flops with no bra, and pull her hair into a sloppy ponytail as she made it to the hotel lobby. While she was walking on her red carpet, Diamond called. She was just about to finally enjoy herself, but she had to answer his call. Anyone else would've gotten her voicemail. He was the only man on the planet that she could not ignore. He was like a brother to her, and she really adored him. They were cut from the same cloth, with different genders but the same heart of gold. He summoned her to meet him for drinks at the hotel bar later that night around 10 o'clock. She agreed and then went on to do some gambling.

Although Kelis was a big gambler, she knew how to sustain it for hours, sometimes days, but once she got started, she couldn't leave the table unless she had broken a heart, the bank, or her pocketbook. A few hours had gone by, and she was now losing more than she intended... 5,000 dollars to be exact. When losing, her mood changes drastically. It's like she becomes someone else, someone not so nice! In the midst of all of this, her only focus is trying to win her money back. His timing was imperfect, and right now, even Diamond could go to hell.

The bar around the poker table was filled with mostly men and a few women. Many of the women were working girls or mistresses. Out of nowhere, a waitress came to her with a drink from someone anonymous. Who was observing her intensity so much that she thought she needed a drink? That kind of attention weighed heavily and that is when she got up from the table. Kelis knew what kind of gambler she had become and realized how uncomfortable she felt when someone visualized the depths of it. Suddenly, she grabbed two five-hundred-dollar chips from the table and sat at the end of the bar. She felt spotlighted and wanted to be out of eyesight and ear shot of everyone. She barely had one ass cheek on the stool when the waitress walked up to her with a drink from that same anonymous stranger. The second drink came on time since she was trying to get a handle on her emotions. At this point, she was angry but mostly strung out. After a few more shots down, she was cool but knew the night had just started. While sitting, the waitress gave her another drink from her infamous admirer. This time, she refused the offer but sent him one back. When she asked the waitress who was sending the drinks, all she would say was that she was the server, not the observer. "OK, Smart Bitch," Kelis said, "I guess I'll have to do my own investigating." Wow, it was like finding Waldo since there were about 50 men seated around. After sitting there sipping and trying to figure out who the mystery man was, she decided to ask the bartender.

The bartender refused to name names, so he remained tight-lipped. Kelis was convinced that someone there was playing a game and did not know when to stop. The game was cute at first, but now it's coming off quite creepy. Normally, Kelis could judge a player in the dark, but this was Vegas. Here in Vegas, there were many different types of men with different nationalities with their A-game. Everyone here tonight was not bad to look at, even the bartender. No crossed-eyed therapist pouring drinks here tonight and they were all well camouflaged. It was really hard to determine who was the drug dealer, business maker, or heartbreaker!

Sitting in the far right of the bar were three distinguished preserved Great Danes. They were superb eye candy that would give a woman a cavity, so damaging a root canal would be needed. They were professionally dressed, so Kelis assumed they were either there for a wedding, convention, or an occasional boy's weekend. It was an all-you-can-eat buffet, and everything was presented on the menu. She had to warn Miss Kitty to sharpen her claws. Tonight, she was not going to judge men by the number of digits in their bank accounts or what kind of ride they were whipping. Therefore, their age wasn't going to be an issue; just as long as they did not come straight from the playground, they would be doable. Hopefully, she may even find out that young brothers do have more than a hard dick in one hand and a blunt in the other. While savoring her last drink, the bartender handed her a note. It said for her to meet there later again tonight at midnight… "Meet who?" she asked. The game went into extra innings, and she was done playing at the ballpark. She slid the note back to the bartender and said, "No, thank you." Whoever sent those drinks played the game too long and she was now bored as hell. Bartenders are not only therapists, but they are also skilled accomplices if given a good tip. Kelis was done with playing hide & seek, and if Diamond did not call soon; he too would be playing hide & seek to find her. Her mind was still at the Poker table and all she wanted to do was try to win her money back. Time spent at the bar was just a slight detour and really a waste of time. No money was made, and the only thing given was probably a hangover in the morning.

Finally, Diamond graced her with his presence, but he was not alone. He was with another grey-haired handsome gentleman. His name was Cordell Wilkerson. Mr. Wilkerson was a Dominican real estate developer. His company was responsible for designing and owning many prestigious buildings throughout the country. He was rich, gorgeous, and very sexy. They were replicas of one another and only their age difference divided them. Shortly after Diamond introduced Kelis to Mr. Wilkerson, it all came together. She knew he was contemplating a new lifestyle, but she had no idea; he was thinking about playing for the other team. Diamond was a businessman. If it took fucking men to big up his brand, then so be it. His motto was… 21 to 80, cripple blind, crazy and all major credit cards are accepted!

After several more shots, the sun roused and smothered the night. They were not all done for the evening, but preserved what was left for later. Kelis was staying on the 10th floor of the Bellagio, while the private elevator to their suite was located opposite of the hotel. As Diamond and Mr. Wilkerson escorted Kelis to the elevator, Diamond knew she had plenty of questions to ask but knew it was not the time. While riding up on the elevator, her mind was on nothing but her bed. She spontaneously laughed out loud because there was a time when the sun came up; it only reminded you how long you were partying.

Last night, Kelis got caught up and was never able to win her money back. She came to Vegas in search of herself and wanted to find out who was really in control. The odds of winning are provided somewhere in the universe.

PS. THE ONLY SURE THING IN LIFE IS DEATH AND TAXES.

CHAPTER 24

MR. WINSTON TISDALE

It was now 2 o'clock in the afternoon, and Kelis had awakened by another hangover. Hangovers are becoming the new norm, especially when the cause of them is headlined. Last night's surprise was the only thing that was trying to compete with her headache. Some say another drink will end your suffering, but the thought of taking another shot of anything seems impossible. Most of the morning, she was kissing the toilet, but what was trying to come up finally did. It was about 4 o'clock in the afternoon before she was feeling much better and was able to eat something.

All morning since she had awakened, Kelis had been thinking about Diamond and tried to call his phone several times but got no answer. Once she got into the shower, her phone rang. However, she was soaking wet and did not want to risk falling on those marble floors, so whoever was calling had to wait. Quickly after her shower, she finally checked her phone, and it was Diamond returning her call.

Suddenly, there was a knock on the door. This time, she went to put a robe on, and there would be no free glances. When she did look through the peephole, it was not the concierge with flowers... it was Diamond. When he entered, he reeked of Hennessey, not of his Gucci cologne. He was still sporting yesterday's clothing and attitude. At first sight, they both hysterically started laughing. Kelis was aware of what was funny but were they both laughing at the same thing? Once the chuckling ended, Kelis turned straight-faced, looking for straight answers. Diamond was a grown-ass man, so she had to choose her words wisely. If not, he could hurt her feelings and tell her to mind her damn business. Turns out he did not have a problem discussing his newfound likeness for dick or a problem fucking men for money. Therefore, since he treats everything like business, there will be no renegotiating or nonrefundable situations occurring. That was introduced to him by a previous lover, and how he would always do his business. Talk about a brother expanding his brand; he took it to a whole new level. After a compelling argument was made, he would not about to label himself gay or bisexual but a good businessman! Before the topic was put to rest, there was just one thing Kelis needed to know. How the fuck they met and who was top or bottom? Diamond said, "OK, Girl, this will be the last time I am going to answer any questions about my affairs."

One day, he met Cordell in Miami while he was spending time with a client. The clients, whom he will not name, are very good friends. He revealed that on the very first time they were introduced, Cordell propositioned him. Diamond immediately shut him down, but Cordell continued to pursue him anyway. Then, one day, he was shopping in Bergdorf, and ran into Cordel. There once again Diamond declined his advances. Two days later three cashmere sweaters were delivered to his apartment, sent by no other than Mr. Cordel Wilkerson. At first Diamond wondered how he knew where he lived but it turns out all you need is someone's name, and they could be found anywhere. As the weeks went by more and more beautiful things were sent to his place and surprisingly a violinist too. Not much else was to say but like all the rest, he was given an offer he couldn't refused and not to mentioned getting his asshole firmly licked.

The last question asked... "Who is the receiver or deliverer?" Kelis asked. "Come on Kelis, does that matter Diamond said? All Kelis could do was shake her head and think, *"Same game, different position played."*

They spent the rest of the early afternoon eating strawberries, and drinking mimosas mixed with the best champagne, complements from Mr. Wilkerson. In the corner of the hotel's floor was a black orchid, Diamond questioned it, but Kelis asked to drop the investigation. "So, what's on the agenda tonight?" Kelis asked. "As a matter of fact, Cordell is hosting a high-stakes poker game in our suite, and I wanted to invite you. There will be some high-profile men attending and Bitch please, dress the part." "Who the fuck are you talking to like that?" she said. "No disrespect, Kelis; I mean, wear something classy and elegant; leave those tight-ass jeans in the closet," he said. "Fuck you, Diamond, I am nobody's walking billboard," she said. Kelis knew how to dress appropriately, when necessary, but she, too, couldn't wear her jeans any tighter. "Calm down, Heffer; all I am saying is to wear something sexy but not trashy. Take it from me, men do like a little mystery, but today, you girls think that a big ass is all that is required. Just remember, Kelis, every other woman today is a 'Build A Bear,' and it's hard to tell the difference between the real or the fake." "That is so true, but only fake niggas, like fake asses," she said. "Really, Kelis, looking back, you have always had a cute shape, but where did you get all that ass?" "My ass is authentic; check my DNA; my grandmother always had an hourglass figure and an ass shaped like an onion since coming here from South Carolina at the age of 17 years old." "Oh yeah, thank goodness you took your grandmother's genes in the body because Asian women have flat asses," he said. "Really, but with their hair texture and eye definition, both genes created one bad bitch," she said. "OK, you're right, but who is the blame for that nasty attitude?" he asked. After going back and forth, neither took anything personally and actually had some fun ribbing each other. There you have it: two good friends having a clean fight and still loving each other thereafter. Diamond vacated the premises and Kelis spent the rest of the afternoon relishing the night ahead. Diamond presented a good case for himself, but she knows better.

Sometime that afternoon, she received a call from Suki before taking a late nap. He was considering coming to Vegas for a few days and she immediately shut him down. She had not been in Vegas for a whole day, and he already wanted to come and disrupt her peace. After convincing him to stay his ass in Brooklyn, the subject of what she was wearing tonight came up. There was not much to select from but that cute black dress she bought yesterday definitely fitted the bill. Black was a good color but not necessarily a good match up against her dark skin. Black-on-black crime was disgraceful, and when the color was laid up against her complexion it was just as ugly! The only thing Kelis liked in black were her men and orchids. Suki convinced her that if she wore the dress, a white gardenia flower should be worn in her hair to add some light to all that darkness. Taking fashion notes from Suki is smart because his talent is so amazingly spectacular. The anticipation for tonight's agenda to occur, was like waiting for Christmas to arrive. Just the thought of gambling tonight filled her lungs with so much air that it made her feel like she was about to fly. So, her mission in life was to keep her lungs filled and her heart protected.

In the meantime, she decided to get a spa treatment. Her room came with complimentary spa accommodations, but you had up to 3 o'clock to make an appointment. On her way down on the elevator, three women dressed in Hijab eyeball her intensively. They observed her through their head covering and she did through her shades. Their Hijab was woven in imported silk, and they smelled like pure money. No disrespect to Muslim women around the world. She definitely knew these women were probably from Qatar, Luxembourg, or even Dubai. They rocked beautiful diamonds, gold jewelry, and very expensive handbags. The elevator ride stopped on almost every floor, and when one got off, more entered. At least 10 Muslim women surrounded Kelis.

Suddenly, one of the women spoke. Their question to Kelis was where she originated from. Looking around the elevator, she felt that was a personal question, but she was outnumbered, so she obliged. She said she was African American, but her father was Asian. Questioning her identity was necessary because of her toasted skin tone and Chinky eyes had them guessing. Once the elevator reached the 3rd floor, everyone had evacuated. Kelis was amongst the group, and it seemed like they all were heading to the same place. It was obvious that they were all scheduled for a spa treatment but what kind of treatment were these women getting? Unless they were only getting a facial or their nails and toes done, Muslim women do not disrobe themselves for anyone but their husbands.

Once inside the spa, Kelis was politely informed that since she did not have an appointment, she would not be able to be accommodated. One of the women overheard the conversation and pulled some strings, and before she knew it, Kelis was knee-deep in avocado scrub. Somebody around here got some clout, and it only took five minutes to showcase it! Surprisingly, the women were really nice. It was very unexpected of them to show that kind of decency. That is why you should never judge a book by its cover!

Long ago, Asians dominated most of the population in Dubai, but now it is mixed with Indians, Pakistanis, and Emiratis. Whatever nationality they believed she was, she was it for the moment, but don't let anyone else get it fucked up... Black coffee, no sugar, no cream! It was now going on 6 o'clock, and those people at the spa worked every kink out of her body. The facial and pussy wash were also the shit.

Once she got back to her room, Diamond continued to be a nuisance by calling multiple times. She could tell by the way, he was slurring his words, she knew he was still drunk. He had the audacity to question her whereabouts. This was coming from a man who never lets anyone know where he lives. He started jabbering about Kelis's tardiness and having too many shots. Lately, he has been calling her more than usual. I guess having a man in your bed isn't as satisfying as depositing checks. Kelis began to wonder how long it was going to take him to get tired of selling his soul for money. It has not been that long since he has been around women or remember that we take our time, when necessary if not always.

The Sapphire Suite was at an entirely different part of the hotel, and a key code was needed in order to get on the elevator. Kelis was without a key and had lost communication with Diamond. "Oh well, this night will not be a waste, nor will this outfit." On her way to the tables, she started her own neighborhood watch but found out someone was already tenant patrolling. He was a well-seasoned Caucasian man. He nodded his head, and two waiters entered her space. She was given two menus, one for drinks and the other for appetizers. She was very impressed, who said "White Man Can't Jump." Kelis was no longer impressed with those who bought the drinks but who owned the distill. After she devoured two orders of shrimp cocktail and downed 6 shots of Henny, her benefactor started heading towards her. Just when he was about to introduce himself, Diamond called. He told her to hurry because the game was about to start and for her to immediately head towards the private elevator. Out of nowhere, a French concierge escorted her to the golden doors. Without hesitation, she left and did not even say thank you nor goodnight to the friendly Caucasian White man.

The elevator ride went straight up to the Sapphire Suite and when the doors opened, so did her mouth! She thought Sasha's condo was the best she had ever seen, but the private suite at the Bellagio made Sasha's place look like the project. The doors opened to a room filled with well-dressed men and luring sweet sounds of Billie Holiday. The shuffling of cards was serenaded in the background, along with the smell of expensive cognac and cigars. She was handed a cute drink immediately as she got off the elevator and it was definitely not Hennessey. Once inside, she immediately took a seat by the window. After observing the crowd for about 30 minutes, the very same Caucasian gentlemen she rudely dismissed downstairs at the poker table sat right next to her. He introduced himself as Mr. Winston Tisdale. He was a Diplomat, that traveled to Vegas for a little relaxation. Diplomats are responsible for overseeing international relations to create peace for various cultures and countries. Finally, Kelis's anonymous stranger was revealed. He was intrigued with her the minute he saw her walk into the hotel on the very first day of her arrival. Diamonds instrumented this entire introduction.

Everything about tonight focused on the nonexistent poker game and to think it was all because a rich, powerful man wanted to get some pussy.

Since he had gone to so much trouble, she decided his efforts were worth at least a conversation. Unexpectedly, she found him to be very interesting, not corny or boring. He asked very few questions and allowed her to do most of the talking. He hung on to her every word and seemed to be interested in everything she had to say. Kelis had her share of men, but never had she been around one that was more interested in her thoughts than her anatomy. White people were always considered the enemy, but times are different now. Like her grandmother once said, all men are created equal; she was not thinking about the human race but the male species. She wondered if it was his nationality or the way he articulated his words when he spoke. He was very well groomed, down to his clean-manicured fingernails and barely scuffed shoes. No matter how powerful, his willingness to walk alongside people showed his humanity. For the first time in her life, she was cultivated by someone's intellect and that really turned her on. He was gentle, non-abrasive and spoke four different languages fluently. Although this man came wrapped nicely, her intention was to do him like the rest! Kelis did not care whose bow was the biggest; she always considered herself the ultimate prize! Furthermore, she was in Vegas, and everything she dreamt was going to happen was happening. PS... I HOPE HE KNOWS THAT WHATEVER HAPPENS IN VEGAS, DOESN'T NECESSARILY HAS TO STAY IN VEGAS.

CHAPTER 25

LIFE WITH MR. WINSTON TISDALE

It's been three years since Kelis and Winston met in Vegas and ever since, she has been on top of the world! They spent most of their time traveling. With all there was to see, she was missing Brooklyn. Her desire to go back home confused him since places like the Maldives and Dubai were so much more captivating. Kelis learned that Winston was a man out of touch with life's personal endeavors. He never married nor had children and was so disconnected from bonding with family. Men like him, who put their careers first, become obsessed with superficial things. At the same time, his unwillingness to identify made him live vicariously through other people's lives. That just goes to tell you that no matter where you go in this world, there is nothing like home.

Sometime that year, Kelis had gotten pregnant and had an abortion without informing Winston. He was livid, but not necessarily because she aborted the baby but because she handled the situation without informing him. When confronted, Kelis applied... my uterus, my choice! Many women today would have loved to have been in her shoes. Trapping a rich guy by purposely getting pregnant was not the route Kelis was taking. Although those biscuits would've been well buttered, she wasn't ready for any to pop out of her oven. Aborting his child was the first of many things that shook their foundation and led to the demise of this relationship. All her life, she thrived to get to a place where she wanted for nothing. Finally, when she was able to live that life, all she wanted was to go back to Brooklyn, and sit on her grandmother's stoop. As she looks back, those were not just cemented steps, it was her throne. For most of her life, she ran the streets in an attempt to make a lot of money to support some unhealthy habits.

Yes, a lot of money was made, but so much of it was lost to gambling and partying. Over the years, she learned that you cannot give back time or money spent. She realizes that her beauty was her only calling card and that, in time, it would expire. She was aware that she was getting older and Mr. Winston's infatuation with her was sand slowly emptying out of an hourglass. She always believed: A BEAUTIFUL OLDER WOMAN IS LIKE A WELL-CARED FOR VINTAGE CAR. ALTHOUGH HER COAT STILL REMAINS SHINY AND HER ENGINE STILL PURRS LIKE A KITTEN. SHE HAS WAY TOO MUCH MILEAGE AND WOULD SOON BE TRADED IN FOR A NEWER MODEL!

When Kelis left Brooklyn, she left knowing she had a problem, but instead she spread her wings in Vegas in hopes of doubling her money, adding more copper to her complexion, and if all fails, start all over again. Winston was not trying to understand her desire to go back to Brooklyn. To him, Brooklyn was where her life ended and with him is where it began. The thought of leaving all of what he was giving behind was scary, but she was no longer happy. She was an adrenaline junkie, and he and the things he provided no longer had her adrenaline going. Since Winston was a Diplomat, he was often accompanied by at least three security agents. Although Kelis was also raised around some form of security, she was tired of intrusiveness. She understood the need for tight security, but cameras were everywhere, including their bedroom. Only a freaky, paranoid person would place cameras where they shouldn't be, so she continued to go along with his fetish for cameras. Nonetheless, he replied, "My house, my rules!"

As time went on, he became more controlling, and she was beginning to feel like a hostage. It had been a while since she started feeling like that and that is when she began to prepare her exit. Every week a certain amount of money was put into her bank account. That was easy to do since Winston paid all the bills and her money was for her pleasure. The only money that was never questioned was what she won at those high-stakes poker games, so that was the money she saved. Other than that, anything major purchased had to be approved by him or his accountant. Furthermore, Winston was cool, but she was bored and wanted to go back to where she belonged... good old Brooklyn.

Night fell quickly and she was informed by Winston's assistant that plans had changed, and he would be arriving a couple of days later because of bad weather. He was coming in on a private plane and it was seriously advised to do so. Most times, upon returning from his trips, he insists that Kelis wait up for him, but tonight, she was really tired and decided to go to bed early. Sometime later that night, she heard a loud thump and through her peripheral, Winston was standing over. Her. When he realized she was not asleep, he leaned over and gave her a kiss. It turns out the pilot was cleared to fly the plane, and that is why he was able to come home early as planned. Naturally, a nice kiss is always presented upon his return, along with something beautiful from Tiffany's or the Louis Vuitton store. Surprisingly, he had come empty-handed, and it seemed like he had done it intentionally.

An hour had passed, and so did the moment and Winston was now in the shower. Kelis decided to take the moment to rehearse what she was going to say to him about her decision to go back to Brooklyn. Once he got out of the shower a much quieter man emerged. Sitting upright on the edge of the bed, ready for war, Winston pulled Kelis up close. He was definitely in the mood to fuck and so was she. As he began to go down between her legs, she allowed the man to take charge. There was not much for her to say or complain about since he was teasing the hell out of her clitoris. Winston was a man that enjoyed a woman's bottom and when he was done lashing on that pussy, he started on other parts of her body. He was a Caucasian man, and all those myths about White men having small dicks and no game in bed is a damn lie. His ability to slay was one of the reasons Kelis hung around as long as she did because although he paid like he weighed, that dick was heavy like a mother fucker.

After a night of getting her pussy demolished, Kelis had awakened early, but unexpectedly, Winston had gotten up earlier. He was on the balcony watching the sunrise when she approached him from behind in a playful mood. The morning had brought on a surprisingly different attitude and was not surprised by her mood swings. Just when she was about to ease up behind him, he turned around and in his hands was a small velvet box. Entering the balcony, she never noticed how beautifully things were arranged. There were bouquets of flowers and many bottles of champagne chilling nearby. Down below, a violinist was playing and rose pedals were everywhere on the lawn. Immediately, she knew where all this was going but proceeded to open the box anyway. Laying so comfortably on a black velour was a ten-carat pear-shaped diamond ring. The reflection of the sun danced off its stone and it nearly blinded all in its presence. By then, Winston was down on one knee, and before he could ask Kelis to marry him, she interrupted him. Before a word could come out of his mouth, she shot him down. He got very angry and immediately went off the balcony to the other joining room. She then ran after him, to try to explain but he then called security. During that time, she begged him to listen, but he was so in his own feelings that he selfishly wouldn't allow her to state her case. Her rejection blew him away because he believed that any woman from where she came from should be overjoyed, overwhelmed, and over the moon because of his caliber. That's what he believed, and that is what he said that morning, so would the real bigot stand up? At that moment, Kelis did not see a hurt man; she saw a prejudiced man. So, for the rest of the morning, she stood out of his way, and he stood out of hers. All her things were viciously thrown in the back of a truck like garbage. His security team was moving so fast that she made sure she got out of their way before they threw her out as well. After a while, the place got quiet, and all that was heard was the splashing of the ocean. That kind of shit made Kelis very nervous because the noise gave her an idea of what was going on.

Instantly doors started slamming, and she sat quietly waiting for instructions. After about two hours had passed with nothing to eat or drink, Winston finally came to the room and walked right past her. He then took a few more steps in her direction and purposely dropped a note on the floor. She slowly picked it up and it read…

PLEASE BE PREPARED TO VACATE THE PREMISES IMMEDIATELY. DO NOT TAKE ANYTHING THAT DOES NOT BELONG TO YOU. YOUR CELL PHONE, POCKETBOOK AND TINY BLACK DRESS I MET YOU IN IS ALL YOU ARE ALLOWED TO TAKE WITH YOU. MY SECURITY TEAM WILL BE ESCORTING

YOU TO THE AIRPORT WITHIN AN HOUR. YOU WILL BE GIVEN ONE HUNDRED DOLLARS. HOPEFULLY THAT WILL BE ENOUGH TO BUY YOU SOMETHING TO EAT WHILE WAITING ON YOUR FLIGHT. ALSO, THE REST IS FOR YOU TO TAKE ANUBER FROM THE AIRPORT, SO YOU COULD GET BACK TO YOUR SANTUARY... BROOKLYN! At first, she thought it was a joke, but when she was given her cell phone and that black dress, she knew shit was real. She hollered out loud to Winston but got no response. She was given five minutes to vacate and not fifteen minutes and not a minute more.

Bali was very hot, and that tiny black dress would suffice, but he knew when she got off the plane in New York, her ass was going to freeze. She then quickly jumped into that very tiny dress that she hadn't worn in two years and immediately tried to call Sasha, but her cell phone had no bars. She politely asked Winston if he could charge her phone, but he nastily said... you wanted your cellphone; having it not fully charged was not his problem. Still so confused and caught off guard, she began to cry. So, unbothered by her tears, he threw her out of his home, with just that tiny black dress on and flip flops.

He assigned two men from his security team to escort her to the airport. The flight from Bali to New York took 22 hours, and that was like 22 months to Kelis. She was angry, cold and tired but she was finally going home. Realistically, Kelis was not surprised by Winston's behavior, only by hers. Winston never had her fooled and from the very first day she left for Vegas, she knew it was going to be an adventure. However, instead of Vegas, she should've gone to get some help for her problem. Being able to live the life most people dream of was worth it to her, but now that she had the taste of the good life, there was no going back to scraps. Somehow, she wanted to make things happen for herself.

PS. INDEPENDENCE IS A BEAUTIFUL THING, ITS PRICELESS AND FREEING AND IT GIVES YOU ENDLESS POWER.

CHAPTER 26

FAMILY REUNION

As her plane touched down at JFK airport, Kelis automatically knew she was home. If blindfolded or deaf, she still would be able to feel its vibe. As she walked through the corridor, flip-flopping along, wearing a tiny dress, Sasha's face was the first thing she saw. Sasha showed up with Cruising and although Kelis had been gone a while, she had forgotten how fine he was. Sasha was sporting a new hairstyle and had put on some contentment weight. Whether it was happy fat or too much cheesecake fat, she was looking damn good.

Nevertheless, a few pounds don't hurt anyone unless you are too many pounds overweight already. Along with that happy weight, she brought to the curb a bad ass Mercedes AMG S63. Seems like some things may have changed, while other things remained the same. Sasha was still looking out for her friend; along with everything else, she brought Kelis a floor-length mink and a pair of Ugg boots. Leaving Bali, she was dressed for their temperature, not for New York. Lamping in the back of her AMG S63 brought back memories of their High School years. The music was blasting just as loud, and Sasha was still back seat driving.

There was plenty to talk about, but Kelis wanted to wait until they both were alone to talk about her shit. Since Kelis was a no show to the podium, Sasha took the stage to narrate hers. She had recently enrolled in college and was taking some business courses. She and her father were in a better place, and she was also interning at his office. Kelis was so happy to hear that, since family meant everything to her. The first stop she wanted to make was at her grandmother's house. When they pulled up to the yard, it was filled with so much debris. Sasha was given a spare key to occasionally come by and check on things. That was such a good idea since Kelis is without a key to the house or anything else. When entering, the key invaded the lock, and suddenly the door opened. Once the door finally opened, the smell of mildew and mothballs caught their nose. The house was very cold, and the rooms were dark and saddened with emptiness.

No electricity or gas was on, so after a quick walkthrough, they were forced to leave. Sasha offered Kelis to stay at the condo, and she agreed, but she wanted to go see Porsche. These days, Porsche has found a brand-new way to get paper. She has learned how to inject silicone into women's asses. While in Miami getting work done herself, she met a girl named Marquette. She was from the Dominican Republic and she and Porsche has gotten together and made a big name for themselves. Over the last year, Suki has been keeping Kelis on what was going on back home. He occasionally did mention Porsche's new business but never mentioned that he was also a client. Same old Suki running his mouth but leaving what part he has also played in it. Speaking of Suki, Kelis had thoughts of going to see him and the children. Her first day back, she wanted to go see everyone, but she started feeling jetlagged. When she called Suki and told him that she was back in town and wasn't going to stop by until tomorrow, he put the children on the phone. Oh, why does he play dirty? Kelis was able to say no to Suki but wouldn't dare say no to her god kids. Had they not been who she remembered; Kelis would not have recognized them. Jada was still a cute little thing, and she was maturing. Her body development wasn't developing too quickly but her blueprint was in the making. Now that Jade was finally coming out of his shell, those million-dollar speech lessons were money well spent. He was no longer stuttering and talked with a lot of confidence. It's clear to see he was indeed Suki's child! Being there tonight, with a lot of bullshit going on, seeing the kids was what she needed. No more looking through the rear-view mirror and she was not going to be part of a pity party. Oh yes, her plans had failed, but she was back in Brooklyn, her old stomping grounds, still cute and a whole lot smarter. The day was beginning to wind down and she was beginning to feel that jetlagged creeping upon her again. Sasha was still enjoying herself and not ready to leave, she used that time to take a nap. While napping, someone licked her cheek. She immediately swiped at it, thinking it may be one of the Dalmatians. No, it was an entirely different type of dog... Bleu. Yuk, when this Negro started licking bitches faces, she wondered. So, not impressed by his gesture or presence, Kelis kindly rolled over. Bleu, being there, has Suki's name all over it. When will Suki give up on this fantasy of them ever getting back together? Since Bleu, Kelis has flown to about 10 different countries and dined at restaurants neither of them could pronounce and has gotten everything she has ever wanted without asking. Indeed, all that sounds divine, but as we all know, Kelis was not happy with Winston nor Bleu. However, she loved her friends dearly, but she was sick of them always trying to play matchmaker. They always felt she needed to be tamed, and somehow, a man was going to be able to do that. No man alive was able to control her, and she didn't care how much money they had; she was a different kind of beast that needed to do her own thing and be free. It was good to see everyone, Bleu too, but it was time to go. Her next stop was going to see what was up with her aunt, Porsche. Hanging with her crew was nice, but times have changed. They all were at different places in their lives, but unfortunately, Kelis had not found her place yet. Tomorrow morning, she plans on definitely going to see Porsche. She recently bought a condo in Queens. Traveling out there could be stressful for any driver since one address is attached to three areas: Avenue, Street, and Place. Thank goodness she'll be taking an Uber, and that will be the driver's problem.

Finally, the night ended, and everyone went on their way with the same redemption of who Kelis was. I guess they believed that by her being away for a while, she might've felt different about some things. Kelis vowed to never change anything about herself, but the number of digits in her bank account and the amount of mother fuckers, she continues to not fuck with. Back at the condo, it was good to finally take a shower and lay down. Sasha came into her room to catch up on their much-needed talk, but by then, Kelis was fast asleep.

The sun rose by 6:30 and Kelis was already dressed and on her way to her auntie's apartment. Before she left, she went by Sasha's room and noticed through the cracked door that she and Cruising were locked in each other's arms, blissfully sleeping. She said to herself, *"Now that is a beautiful sight."* A tear took hostage in the corner of her eye, and she thanked God that happiness had come to her friend. How is it that a person could want happiness for others but seem to destroy it for themselves? After nearly going through all five boroughs, the dumb-ass Uber driver finally found her aunt's apartment complex... those damn Queen Streets. As the cab pulled up to this cute little Highrise, Kelis couldn't help but smile. Porsche has always given her a different vibe on how she would live, and this place here in Queens is far from what Kelis envisioned. The entry to the complex was not as fly as the condos in Manhattan but it had its own spin. The foundation of the building was strong and also very clean. The fact that it was clean sold on her. Surprisingly, when addressing the front desk, Kelis's name was listed on the call log. Therefore, no introduction was needed to get into the building, just proper identification. When she got off the elevator, she went to apt# 6B, but before she could knock, Porsche opened the door quickly, and they both hollered and embraced each other tightly. The warm reception from her aunt was what she really needed, especially when she left for Vegas two years ago. They were not on the best of terms. No takeaway from friends, but Porsche was family, so you already know the rest. Her apartment was cuter inside, very clean, and sterile like with not much furniture. She had three bedrooms, hers completely furnished, but the other two rooms looked like an infirmary. There were no signs of life in either room, whereas in the rest of the house, displayed pictures of the family. There were plenty of questions to be asked, but so much time had passed, and Kelis did not want to start things off by pushing sensitive buttons. Porsche was looking good and seemed to be doing OK. She was turning forty years old this year, and Kelis believed that was mainly the reason for her drastic life turnaround. For the rest of the morning, they reminisced on only things that made them laugh and nothing that made them cry. Sometime after their third mimosa, the doorbell rang. It was a tall transgender with a porcelain face of a goddess. Porsche introduced Kelis to her, and she went by the name of China, of course. After a quick introduction, Porsche ushered her into one of the sterile rooms down the hall and closed the door. It took all of five minutes when Porsche came out, closing the door behind, saying China needed to lay still for a couple of hours.

"Needed to lay still for what?" Kelis asked. Porsche then looked at Kelis as if she was stupid and said, "You know what I do?" "No, I do not know what you do," Porsche said. "Don't tell me that your nosey ass friend didn't tell you how I was getting money these days." "OK, yes, he did, but you know I try not to believe everything Suki says." That's when all the rumors were addressed, and oh boy was it a doozy. Porsche was making money injecting silicone into people's asses. She had a clientele larger than life, and many of them were well-known celebrities. Turns out the condo was her business office, and her real home was in Brooklyn Heights. The bitch owned a million-dollar brownstone, three luxurious cars and owned four funeral parlors. Her aunt Lexus had made an empire on silicone injections and every bitch from the Hood to Hollywood knew her work. Kelis was impressed by her aunt's business savvy but did not like the dangerous flip side of it. So, she was not going to hate but congratulate. Time brought on a change and somewhere in Heaven, her grandmother was smiling down, hopefully not so worried but relieved that her girls had learned to respect each other and one another's hustle. Since Kelis's return, everyone seems to be doing well and living their best life. At the same time, Kelis was still searching for something that may or may not even exist.

PS. (BLACK GIRL LOST) STILL IN SEARCH OF HERSELF.

CHAPTER 27

BLACK GIRL LOST

A week had passed, and it was time for Kelis to get on with her life. The reunions were nice but talking about the past shed no light on her future. Last on her list of people to get acquainted with was her favorite aunt, Mercedes. She had called early that morning, and they talked too late that noon. Mercedes was doing well interning at Mount Sinai hospital in Chicago. There is where she met her fiancé, Muhammad Desir. He is Arabic and just graduated from Med school. He is on his way to becoming a cardiologist. Talk about luck; she left to pursue her studies and got a doctor along the way. Kelis was so happy about her aunt's success and was not surprised by how things turned out for her, considering good things come to those who believe and deserve it! Much of what was going on with Kelis was already discussed, thanks to Porsche's big mouth. Being the aunt that she was, she had to remind Kelis that habits would not be broken if you did not care to deal with them. Many were familiar with Kelis's addiction but acted like it didn't exist. It was quite understood how she got this way and nobody else understood more than her two aunts. Talks of going to Rehab are now brought up more than ever. Her aunt Mercedes offered Kelis to come stay with her in Chicago, but she was not about to go away since she had just gotten back home.

Nevertheless, she was forever grateful but was only interested in making moves in her chosen direction. Suddenly, Kelis received a phone call from Smutty Low. Smutty ran numbers for the Italians back in the day. He also sold liquor to her grandmother dirt cheap. He was an old Gee that never got tired of the streets. He was illiterate but knew how to count money. If not for the number business extinction, he would still be walking the streets and going door to door taking numbers. He blamed it all on the government and when they found a way to capitalize on it, that's when illegal numbers became legit. Thanks for some of the few Spanish bodega in the neighborhood that still makes it possible for our people to still bet on numbers with a better return. Just head to the back of any one of their stores, order some red beans & rice, then drop a $1 on 325 and pray it comes out. These days, he relies on gambling for a quick come-up, along with selling a little smack. The dope business would be just as plentiful for him, but he was his biggest customer. In between times, he was always up for a good dice or a Pity Pat game.

He heard she was back in town and had called to inform her about a new spot in Staten Island. He told her that on any given night, there were plenty of cats playing hardball, and there was plenty of money to be gotten. She had what it took to make her day or somebody else's. All bets were on Kelis, but who the fuck, he thought he was talking to. Just like that, she had to cuss him the fuck out, talking to her as if he was her P.I.M.P. In the midst of their conversation, she wanted to decline because she was used to gambling with diplomats, lawyers, and doctors. The thought of going back to gamble with broke mother fuckers was something she did in High School. Beggars couldn't be choosey, and since she has been back in town, all she has been doing is attending family reunions. Hanging out with Smutty Low and his goonies isn't what Kelis was used to anymore, but in order to get ahead sometimes, you may have to go backward. Not to stay there but to revisit and refresh your mind on what is.

The night had its own agenda, so she decided to go back to the house and see what it would take to get it back the way it used to be or better. When she got there, a Louis Farrakhan-looking character came from behind the bushes. He was hiding alongside the house, and he quickly handed her trespassing papers, jumped in a black Limousine, and speedily drove off. The papers were filed three days ago, and the original owner (Winston Tisdale) would have her arrested if she did not vacate the premises. She immediately called Sasha so that her father could look into the matter. Turns out, not only was the paperwork legit, but her name was not listed on the ownership or the deed. Suddenly, it all came to her, and she became sickened by its acknowledgment. The last time she visited the house, she was able to hear her grandmother's voice, along with the sight of Ms. Remsen sitting in the window, nosing down on folks on the block.

The kind of neighborhood Kelis grew up in has become extinct because children don't come out and play hopscotch or Double Dutch anymore. Children today are being entertained by cell phones and reality TV, but the reality is they are being robbed of their childhood. That was not the case for Kelis; she, too, was robbed of a childhood, not because she did not want to play with other children but because she wasn't allowed. Just when she could not have been more surprised by his actions, something else is proven more of his depths. Talking to Sasha's father, Kelis explained to him that she had signed the new ownership papers. Sasha's father explained that a man like Winston has the power to create any form of document. He was able to change Kevin on her birth certificate rather than Kelis, if he wanted to. She was knocked down again but not out. The whole time, Winston remained the original owner, and the documents he had her signed were fraudulent. For the first time, she would admit, she felt played and made a fool of. Since that incident in Bali, that was a trip to Disney World compared to losing her grandmother's home. She was caught off guard because her mind was on nothing but gambling. Losing the house was like a family member dying. Plenty of blame was passed around, mainly towards Porsche. She was in charge of the mortgage payments, but Kelis later understood that Porsche was busy getting her own life together. The family business was not a priority for her anymore since she was making a boatload of money. Porsche was doing her own thing and so was Kelis.

When Kelis left for Vegas, she also asked Sasha to come through from time to time to be her eyes and ears. When things got crazy in both their lives, they both relied on one another to be that person. When the job was passed down to Kelis, she was so deeply involved in gambling that she just assumed Winston would handle that like he had handled everything else. In the beginning, Winston tried to make things easier for Kelis, but the only thing he made easier was her ability to get more money when needed. The separate accountant was for the mortgage, along with other accountants for her personal needs. Once Winston realized that she wasn't handling business, he had her name removed from not only his bank accounts but also the deed. Winston bankrolled all of Kelis 'needs, and the gambling thing was the first to be sponsored. So, when the bank contacted him about foreclosure in binding, you could imagine how furious he was. Without a mere sign of anguish toward her, he went about business like he always did. It was another day in the neighborhood when a woman put all her eggs in one basket and got an egg on her face. After leaving Sasha's father's office, she went back to Porsche's crib. She had one hundred dollars in her bank account, so broke she couldn't even afford an Uber ride. It's been years since she had ridden the train, and she really wasn't trying to do so, but she was not about to let anyone know just how fucked up she was. When she finally showed up at her aunt's apartment, her aunt was conducting business. Two girls were waiting in the foyer while one was lying down in the room recovering. Kelis was not against women altering their bodies, but most of the women were so young, and they never gave their bodies time to mature. She too often wonders what the future holds, but Kelis believes she has time. Unfortunately, time waits for no man or any woman's body when deflating. So curious and desperate to know how Porsche was making her money, she tiptoed down the hall. Once she got to the room, she eased the door open. There in the room was Porsche injecting silicone into a woman's ass cheek. Minutes later, the woman's ass swelled up like a can of Pillsbury dough biscuit popping out of the can. The woman was in so much pain, and there was blood all over the bed. Needles was something Kelis was afraid of and at the mere sight, she nearly passed out. So, weakened by what she had just witnessed, she took her wobbly legs and weak stomach to her aunt's room and lay down. After she had finally gotten herself together, all she could do was sit and wait until Porsche's day was complete. Just when her aunt was finishing up, the doorbell rang, and there were two other women scheduled to get the same procedure.

By late afternoon, her aunt's apartment was like a hospital. All the rooms were filled, and even one of the girls had to recuperate on her aunt's sofa. By late afternoon, every room was filled with women recuperating. Never had she seen anything like this but in the hospital. Her aunt knew what she was doing and getting paid handsomely. Still shocked and amazed, she sat patiently in her aunt's room. Finally, the worst was over, and her apartment was empty and quiet. Knowing her niece the way she did, Porsche came straight out and asked Kelis what was going on. When Kelis told her aunt the entire story, she held off and smacked her face. In an instant, Kelis drew back to retaliate but dropped her hands. Her aunt got straight up in her face and said, "How the hell could you let this happen?" Once upon a time, Porsche was that dumb bitch, that would have allowed a man to control every thought and action, but today, she was on some other shit, making money, kicking ass, and taking names. Somehow, she took Kelis's moment and made it about her, but that was OK; she had come a long way and earned some bragging rights. However, Porsche was furious; she knew her niece had a serious gambling problem, and they both took full responsibility for losing their childhood home. But it's going to take more than taking responsibility, it's going to take their faith in God.

Secondly, when Kelis left for Vegas, she had a nice penny saved but gambling every night and no money coming in, zeroes eventually made an appearance in her bank account. When she was with Winston and he gave her an allowance, she should've sent money home to be saved, because her allowance was practically like someone giving her the key to the mint vault. Once he realized that she was taking money from every account and having problems balancing their bank accounts, that is when he started monitoring shit. "How much money did you have in your personal account before you started fucking it up, Porsche asked? "About half a million dollars," Out of nowhere Porsche leaned in to smack her but instead she grabbed her and gave her a hug. Deep down inside, Kelis wanted to be slapped because she felt she deserved it.

Nevertheless, the damage was done, but Winston was not done until he was done. That was far more than what her aunt wanted to hear. Now it was time for her aunt to take Kelis to school and this was coming from someone Kelis always thought was not that smart. "Listen up, Baby Girl," Porsche said, "the streets are different now and all those people that had our backs are either dead, in jail, or moved on to other pastures. These no-good niggas out here don't get that kind of money you're used to. Also, brothers today aren't breaking their piggy bank for just any bitch anymore. Bad bitches are everywhere and that bad shape and pretty hair you sport, you could buy that now. You had a chance, Kelis, to get away and live the life many of us dream of. So, you're back, glad to see ya, but many of these mother fuckers do not give a fuck! Those days of tricking men, partying, and gambling to dawn, aren't you tired of that?" "You cannot tell me watching a sunrise from a Villa in France, instead of over someone's backyard fence, isn't a different experience," Porsche said. "Yes, it is," Kelis said, "but being able to watch any sunrise, regardless of where I'm at, is all that matters."

Knowing the conversation was going only in the direction she wanted, Porsche shook her head and walked away.

PS. KNOWLEDGE IS POWER, BUT ONLY TO THOSE LOOKING TO LEARN!

CHAPTER 28

OLD HABITS

Old habits are hard to break, especially when you do not believe they exist. Kelis was now, literally homeless and had sold almost everything she had. However, the mere thought of mingling with guys she once hardly spoke to, was not something she looked forward to doing but she had no choice. Rebuilding was going to be difficult, considering she no longer had the hookups or money. Rome was not built in a day, but it was going to take more than that to get shit the way it once was. Having rich friends, you would think a person would have easy access to whatever they needed. Her friends would supply her with whatever she wanted except anything that has to do with gambling. For years, on the surface, she looked like she was living a perfectly fine life. Her bottom wasn't necessarily everyone else's considering; she was still residing in a million-dollar condo, ate very well and occasionally was driven around in some very expensive cars.

After her conversation with Smutty Low, she spent the entire morning pondering ideas on how to get some money to go play cards with him later that night. Desperation is why she called him, and regret is going to call on her. Early that morning, she went to the condo. Sasha had already left for the day, so she was able to walk around freely. There were a few safes in the apartment, but the real money and jewels were locked away. There in the hall was an open safe due to Sasha never remembering the combination. When she finally opened the closet, the safe was gone. At first, she was pissed off but was really mad at herself. She could not believe how desperate she had become. She was disgusted but was still on to her next quest. Just as planned, she met up with Smutty Low on the Avenue and when she jumped into his ride, he was riding dirty. Not necessarily any illegal firearms or paraphernalia, just two dirty niggas riding shotgun. If known, she probably would have walked, but once inside, all she could do was stay quiet and keep an eye on everyone's movement. When asked about his entourage, his car, his rules. In her mind, her thoughts were if it was like that, she could've taken an Uber. His attitude had taken a different tone since their conversation, but she remained cool. It's a shame in the presence of their peers, men like to show out. It makes no sense, but I guess it is a testosterone thing.

The ride to Staten Island must have taken two hours, so I guess these goons don't know how to travel. All this time, she thought only cab drivers didn't know how to drive, but it seemed like it was a man thing. When they finally pulled up to the spot, it was unexpectedly nice and well-taken care of. There were yellow tulips in the yard, guarded by a white picket fence. It kind of reminded her of her grandmother's house. From the outside, it looks like a nice, wholesome family lived there, but oh, what lurks beyond those fences, except for the fact that in order to get to the basement, you had to enter through his home. There were no side doors or hidden secret pass way. Once downstairs, the basement was filled with strangers mixed with some familiar faces. Not many pleasantries were exchanged, but many stares were. She was offered a drink, but since she did not see who poured it, she declined. Kelis was aware that she was in unfamiliar territory, but she was not going to appear scared or look back.

Thirty minutes into the evening, she went to retrieve her own drink; this time, she observed who was pouring and those in the room. Feeling so uncomfortable, which started from those in the car. Not knowing what to make out for the rest of the evening, a not disturb sign was hung, and for the rest of the night, she kept her distance. While sitting far to the left of the room, waiting for shit to jump off, a cute young guy approached her. He introduced himself as Big Mike. Big Mike was once known as little Micky growing up. He was a stranger to Kelis, but in no time, he went into major details about her life, and she finally started piecing shit together. The finalization of the puzzle was when he mentioned Bleu. He also admitted that although he was a young boy, back in the day, he had a serious crush on her. Kelis was known for owning the sidewalk and making it her private red carpet. She was also known for breaking hearts, and it did not matter who or how old you were. He also told a story of how one day she was coming out of the corner store, and whatever fragrance her body soaked up mesmerized him.

For years, he wondered about the name of the fragrance and nearly sniffed a million bottles in search of it. He knew what car she drove and what her favorite color was, determined by the colors he often saw her in. It was like talking to Charlie Brown... waw, waw, waw! What got her attention was when Big Mike mentioned that he once worked for Bleu. He was Bleu's most trusted soldier and when he retired from the game, he handed his whole empire over to him.

"So, you are the little Mikey Bleu talked so highly about," Kelis said. "Yes, the one and only," he said. "Wow, he took you everywhere except our bedroom," Kelis said. "Trust me, in my mind, I have been in your bedroom many times," he said. "OK, be nice now; I'm old enough to be your auntie," Kelis said. "Yeah, but I'm old enough to give that pussy a black eye," he said and walked away! He left her with her mouth and legs wide open.

Thirty minutes had passed and just when she was about to go get another drink, the room had grown to its capacity. Since she was so desperate to play but did not have the proper funds, she continued to sit. When those who were about to play got seated, Big Mike called her to her seat.

Not wanting to embarrass herself, she gestured to him to do him. Big Mike was a young guy but studied people, especially women, well. He knew she did not come prepared, and he practically called her out on it. Kelis arrived thinking there would be some pity-pat players but had no idea most of them were going to be men. Pity Pat is no longer a game for bitches, where our grandmas and aunties play for quarters. Many guys play and some of them leave the game, nearly in tears. As long as the stakes are high enough, it's each man for himself. However, poker was really not her game, but if played, her money needed to be right. She really preferred to play with men because they were easily distracted. So, trying not to be embarrassed, she sat down at the table next to none other than Big Mike. The cards were dealt real fast and just like that, someone went out. Since her money was not as long as she would have liked, she had to borrow from the house. When she gestured, she was stopped by Big Mike. She told him she could get up, but he insisted she stayed seated. Staying seated meant she was still able to play and own his dime. Apparently, Big Mike had plenty of clout and was definitely the man in that room. With so much cheating going on lately, many establishments, such as this, were allowing one dealer for everyone.

Kelis was not familiar with the new customs or the ruling, but in Rome, she had to do what the Romans did. That was all but a lie; you are the one who makes every choice in your life, especially when it comes to your money. All rules were explained, and they should be taken seriously, especially the one that you would be beheaded if caught cheating. As the cards were dealt each time, no pairs or wild cards appeared in her hand. Kelis was having another no-luck moment, and it took all of no time before she was completely broke. They were playing a hundred dollars a hand, sides, and high cards. This is why she knew she needed to come out right, but she was thirsty to play. Coming to a game like this was like going to Vegas with a hundred dollars, impossible! No fret: this is why people borrow from the house. The house-made no issue with her request, but Big Mike wasn't having it, so he then slid a thousand dollars in front of her without question, and the night continued on. Aww shit, as if she wasn't already impressed with this young cutie, he just went ahead and won him a pussy coupon! Multiple drinks later and a few more dollars were given, Kelis was feeling herself and Big Mike. He was talking greasy all night about how long he and his money was. Big dick talk didn't impress Kelis, but that money magic did.

It was now about six o'clock in the morning and the sun was beginning to rise. All those that were still there had headed towards the door, heads hung low and promises of never returning. Smutty was nowhere to be found and Kelis later learned that he had vacated the premises hours ago. Rumors swirled that he had won and got the hell out of there as if he was on fire. Leaving with your winnings is a smart move for a gambler, but leaving without telling her was grimy. Kelis has been around many dirty niggas like

Smutty, and that is why she held on to a couple of dollars. Not enough to retire on the French Riviera but to grab something to eat and get home. As she walked out of the spot, the sunlight doused her sight. Once she was able to peep through its rays, she spotted Big Mike leaning against his pickup truck. The first thing she thought of was a free ride home. He whistled in her direction and made a U-turn. Quickly, she jumped her ass into his truck, and they drove away. While they were driving, he questioned her luck and then her intentions of paying him back. A look of astonishment painted across her face, but a look of I want my money painted on his! She then began to explain how she thought tonight was a freebee, but everyone knows, especially Kelis, that nothing in this world is free. Then he said, "Did you think all that money you rode on me tonight was free?"

"Yes, Mother Fucker, I tried to borrow my own money, but you kept on insisting, so a bitch like me allowed you to do what you obviously wanted to do," she said. "Do what, Kelis?" "Exploit your wealth and power in front of those Nicky Barnes puppeteers," Kelis said. He asked, "Why would an established, well-paid, respected man such as himself need to impress any of those clowns?" "Boy, please, and I do mean that literally! It is a proven fact that men like you make more money than you ever thought you'll have.

After a while, money is not the main drive; people are, especially women! Earlier this evening, you spoke confidently about your childhood crush on me and who you thought I was. Little boy, get in line; almost every man in that room shared or continued to have the same fantasy. This game you ty to run down on me is tiring and immature. I have been with men more powerful than the President and you all have the same weakness, Pussy! Also, material things do not make a woman come, and sometimes not even a big dick. Yes, we send out signals that we are in heaven, but our biggest orgasm is when we fuck ourselves. The road to a woman's heart is simple if only you guys will take the time to study our map. In his quest for direction, he will learn what makes her purr and give her what she wants without her ever having to ask.

Nevertheless, Big Mike was unimpressed with what Kelis was saying, mostly because he was too young to process it. Young men are only good for one thing, and besides the obvious, you demonstrated it tonight.

The ride home was so uncomfortable, and the truck's engine was all you heard. When Big Mike finally arrived at the condo, no goodbyes or thanks were exchanged, just a loud car door slam. Walking into the apartment, Sasha was the first thing Kelis saw when entering. She was stretched out on the sofa and looking very queasy. Before Kelis could take off her shoes, Sasha dashed to the bathroom. Kelis quickly ran after her and when she got in, Sasha was throwing up all over the place. Not knowing what was happening, Kelis asked Sasha if she was drinking. Sasha replied that she wished she had, then she would know what was wrong with her. Kelis then said, "So you weren't drinking or have the flu?" "No, I am perfectly fine, except for being nauseous and lately throwing up only during the mornings." For about five minutes, all Kelis could do was look at her friend and wonder how dumb she could be. Sasha then noticed how she was responding to her and said, "WHAT?" "Kelis then hollered, "Girl, you're pregnant!" "I am not," Sasha said. "OK," Kelis then reached into the bathroom cabinet and took out three home pregnancy tests. "Piss on this Bitch," Kelis said. Sasha grabbed the test and forcefully pushed Kelis out of the bathroom.

While Sasha was in the bathroom, taking her pregnancy test to determine if she was going to be a momma, Kelis received a phone call from Patrick Damone. Patrick was an old friend of Winston who was now residing in Washington, D.C. She met him in Acapulco while on Vacationing. Patrick was into trading stocks and also had a serious gambling habit. On various occasions, when Winston could not accompany her to some poker games, Winston allowed Patrick to escort her. He was very flirtatious and occasionally flirted with her privately and in front of Winston. Secretly, Kelis did find him somewhat attractive but was not stupid to go there. There was a time when fucking friends was a spectator sport, but back then, she wasn't trying to blow a good thing. Let it be known that Kelis played a lot of games, but none that required the ability to figure a man out. There is where she felt she would definitely lose.

PS. SO, HERE'S TO THOSE THAT COULD AND TO THOSE THAT ARE FOREVER IN RECOVERY!

CHAPTER 29

STAYING FABULOUS

Kelis's conversation with Patrick took all of 15 minutes and just like that, she agreed to meet him at an unfamiliar place far away from Brooklyn... the Bronx. Kelis was a sports junkie, so when he asked her to meet him at Yankee Stadium, she was all in. To make this date more spectacular, he offered to have a car service pick her up. Although she would have loved to be driven to the Bronx but riding through traffic on the Major Deegan during this time of day was brutal. It may sound downright crazy but traveling on the 4 train to the Stadium was part of the Yankee experience. Almost every train cart will be filled with die hard Yankee fans. Once there, thousands of fans rush down the train steps and into the park. The ride was quick and before she knew it, she was seated in a 5,000.00-dollar VIP skybox.

This was the first time Kelis had ever visited a Yankee game nevertheless a skybox. It was beautifully designed and filled with all types of people: celebrities, athletes, owners, agents, and mostly groupies. Considering she was dressed for a ball game but still looked as good as any woman in the room. Never did another woman, looked so good in a baseball cap and jeans. While waiting for Winston to arrive, she noticed how celebrities and rich people huddle together. To amuse herself, she started playing head games, trying to identify who bodies were fake or real and who was a man or a woman. She pretty much had the crowd narrowed down, but in the corner to her right, she could not tell if that was Cher or RuPaul. Spontaneously, some fine-ass young athlete came into the room.

He reeked of money and confidence but was very obnoxious. Seems like his attitude did not bother her, because Kelis knew how to roll with the best of them, and rich athletes were not the only ones who had a bad attitude. By the seventh inning stretched, Patrick was still a no-show. So wrapped up in the scenery and the jumbo shrimps, she just chilled. All of a sudden, when she started making conversation with people, she saw Patrick making his way through the crowd. He immediately apologized, but Kelis assured him that it was OK. His absence gave her a moment to be with herself and that is something people need to learn to do. Throughout the rest of the evening, their conversation was suffocated by the roar of the crowd, especially when one of the Yankees made a base hit or hit a home run. Kelis was cool with not being able to have a decent conversation since she was mainly there to see the Yankees play.

Once the game was over and many exited the skybox, she and Patrick were able to get reacquainted. During their conversation, Winston name was mentioned, and Kelis could care less if she ever heard his name again.

Finally, the conversation shifted and his real purpose for this encounter was established. He confessed how he was always attracted to her and out of respect for his friend, he kept it clean. He also mentioned how recently Winston opened up about their breakup and how devastated he was. As he sat blabbering about another man's heartache, Kelis couldn't believe how full of shit he was. Winston and Patrick were cut from the same cloth, and if he thought Kelis was about to believe the bullshit, he is a damn idiot. If not for the endless jumbo shrimps and the newly popped bottle of Don Perion just brought to their table, Kelis would be on the verge of walking out. But not before she could blatantly get to the bottom of why he was really here. Patrick knew he had to grab hold of his balls and shoot his best shot. "Come on, Kelis, are you going to make an old man beg?" he asked. "Beg for what?" Kelis said. "Girl, you know I have been waiting patiently, not necessarily for you and Winston's relationship to fail but indeed waiting!" "I'm not attractive to a man waiting his turn; I love a nigga who knows what they want and go get it," Kelis said. "Come on, Girl, Winston and I are friends and all the mystic you possess; please don't make me go there," he said. "Oh really, stop the bullshit. Obviously, Winston is not your friend if ever, Kelis said. Kelis, "How old are you now?" Patrick asked. "I'm 34, why?" "In this game, 34 is old, and you know it just as much as I do," Patrick said. "So, what the fuck are you trying to say?" Kelis said. "All I am saying is once upon a time, you were in a position to call all the shots, but those lines in your face and ass cheeks aren't as straight anymore.

However, because you are still a pretty woman, many men may overlook some of your flaws, but that mouth and attitude are lethal, and many men would rather take a bullet," Patrick said. "So, why are you at the gun range?" Kelis asked. "I am here, not too far from my hometown, in hopes of having a good time this weekend and perhaps to get some good pussy, Patrick said. "Oh, so you thought I would fuck you because I sat at the skybox, Kelis said. "No, I believe you would have fuck me for a whole lot less, but I was feeling generous today, so I threw in the skybox," Patrick said. She then attempts to smack him in the face, but he grabs her arm and says, "Did I hit a nerve, he said? "He then throws what's left of her shrimps and champagne in the garbage and told her to get the fuck out or did she want to be thrown out of there, like she was thrown out of Winston Villa.

On the ride home, she thought about what Patrick said some insecurities surfaced. Kelis already knew, she wasn't as young as she once was, but she still had some good years left. Patrick's comments about her aging got her thinking about maybe it's time to get some work done. If that was going to happen, she was going to entrust no one other than her aunt Porsche. She was the Queen of body contouring, and her work was exquisite. However, convincing her to take her on as a client will be difficult since she believes Kelis has many years left to make such a serious decision.

P.S. HOW IS IT THAT, WHEN WE RECONIZED A FLAW ON OUR BODIES, WE ARE SO QUICK TO DO SOMETHING ABOUT IT BUT WHEN ITS OUR PERSONALITIES, NEEDING TO BE ADJUSTED, WE TEND TO DO NOTHING ABOUT THAT BIGGEST FLAW.

CHAPTER 30

MANUFACTURED BITHCHES

The ride home from the stadium was long, but watching the Yankees win made riding the iron horse worthwhile. The train ride going home was nothing like the ride coming in because, by this time, the fans were pumped up, and many were now intoxicated. Kelis's head was everywhere, and all her ideas on how to get money were hitting a brick wall. She had decided to go back to her aunt's apartment and ask for another loan. Traveling from the Bronx to Queens was an adventure in itself, but she had no other choice. When she arrived at her aunt's crib, it was business as usual. Three women were lying in the room recovering. They were all literally faced down and ass up for hours! Porsche was about her bread, so when Kelis showed up unannounced, her aunt gave her two choices: either wait patiently in another room or come back at another convenient time. Normally in the past, if someone had of talk to her like that, Kelis would have given them her ass to kiss. Desperation is a game changer; it can make those that never will, do. While waiting in the next room, Kelis got very impatient. The last time she decided to go look around, she almost got grounded. She slowly peeked in the room and surprisingly, she didn't feel faint or squeamish. This time, she was prepared for the worst, but somehow, she observed freely and was quite impressed with the way Porsche had sharpened her skills. Very little blood was exposed, and the woman was in some pain but not agonizing.

Once Porsche was done making her money for the day, she was able to devote the rest of her day to her niece. While they were talking, Porsche recognized the bullshit but allowed Kelis to continue. Lies and more lies were being told, and finally, it became embarrassing. Porsche knew Kelis was there to borrow more money, but she was not about to loan her anymore. If anything, she offered her a job. The way Kelis looked at her aunt, you would have thought she offered her a job cleaning the sewers. Porsche, of all people, understood Kelis's addiction but refused to loan her any more money but instead wanted to teach her how to fish. Teaching her how to fish is more beneficial than handing her fresh fish from the river. Kelis was a fisherman, but her idea of fishing, was tricking men and, lately, family and friends. The job Porsche was offering was for Kelis to handle bookings for her business. The clientele had gotten so large she needed an assistant ASAP! She was too busy injecting and taking care of women in recovery. She also started offering women to come to get weekly massages, and her calendar was clashing.

Her apartment was getting too small because, on any given day, it could have up to 10 women at a time. The much-needed space was a necessity, but moving somewhere else will be a luxury. Where she lived, the tenants mind their business. Comfortability is very important; it makes you sleep better at night. Also, there are a million girls who would take this job in a heartbeat, but you know trust is mainly the reason why I prefer you. Kelis, your family, and we were taught loyalty. Everyone isn't taught that and it sure cannot be purchased from the store. Wow... how times have changed; Porsche is schooling Kelis on shit, but that's how life works sometimes. You never know who could one day make a difference in your life, so remember, never say never! Working for Porsche was not really the issue; it was what the job detailed. Although she contemplated one day getting some work done herself, this part of the situation she wanted no part of. Out of desperation, she accepted the job, but before Porsche made it official, there were some things Kelis needed to know. Besides keeping appointments aligned, she needed to teach her how to clean the area of the injection site. Also, she had to monitor the women closely while in recovery and was given a minor crash course about the procedures.

Silicone injections of the buttocks are a cosmetic procedure in which silicone is injected into the ass cheeks to enhance the size and shape of someone's buttocks. The method of buttock augmentation is considered a form of non-surgical or minimally invasive plastic surgery. Kelis got highly involved with the crash course; then, she wanted to know how long each procedure lasted. Porsche told her that it could last up to six months and that the patient must be given more injections over time in hopes of maintaining its look.

Kelis also wanted to know the side effects and was told that many of the side effects include infection, vascular embolism, nodule formation, skin discoloration, and, if done long-term, stroke or even death. All of those side effects frightened her, but she was going to do what she wanted. Porsche also reminded her that there would be a lot of crying and tears to fill an ocean. What a lot of them didn't know was Kelis was cold-hearted and had no sympathy for something you choose for yourself. As she mentioned earlier in the book, her body was perfect, and no plastic surgery was needed yet. "So, when do you want to start?" Porsche asked. "Maybe next week because I have some other pressing engagements at the moment," Kelis replied. "What is more important than making money?" Porsche asked. "Not a damn thing, but right now, I have some business to take care of,"

Kelis said. "OK, Girl, but come next Friday, your ass better be here at noon," Porsche said. "No problem, Auntie, but in the meantime, can I have a small cash advance?" Kelis asked. "No work, no pay." Porsche meant every word.

When Kelis left her aunt's apartment, she was still looking to get her hands on some cash. Luckily, over the years, she was given some very beautiful expensive jewelry, including a 5-carat diamond tennis bracelet with matching earrings, given to her by Bleu. That was the last piece of jewelry he gave her for her 30th birthday. Much of her other expensive jewelry was tucked away in Sasha's private home safe. Thank goodness these items were in Sasha's possession, or they would have been pawned a long time ago. In that safe the one thing she would never part with was a ring her father gave to her mother. She vowed never to part with it, no matter what. It was always said to invest in good jewelry. When in need of cash, good jewelry is like money in the bank. Before leaving for Vegas, she had all her good jewelry in Sasha's safe, and going over to get it would be like trying to retrieve the Hope Diamond. There will be so many questions, but at the end of the day, it's her shit, and she felt she owed no one any explanations.

CHAPTER 31

BITCH BETTER HAVE MY MONEY

Going to the condo to retrieve her jewelry was like going to Tiffany's Jewelry store and breaking into their vault. Sasha would be standing in court and using whatever ammunition she could to make her reconsider. At this point, Kelis was at the peak of her addiction and wasn't making any excuses about it. The last time they were in a room together, Sasha was throwing up all over the place and about to take a pregnancy test. Over the last few weeks, Kelis has been running the streets and never backed peddled to find out the outcome of her friend's condition. That's what addiction does; it puts you in a world where only your needs exist. Going to the condo will be like a slow walk-through Hell, but thank goodness, Kelis will wear plenty of sunblock. When Kelis entered the apartment, all her jewelry was neatly aligned in a beautiful case. It was on the piano, along with two duffle bags filled with her belongings. Every piece of jewelry she owned was in it, and some things she did not want to take.

Sasha was done with her friend and knew if Kelis had gotten so desperate to pawn her jewelry, it was just a matter of time before she would be on the streets selling her ass. Sasha was now a pregnant woman, and the stress was not going to kill her. She loved Kelis, but her friend was on a road of destruction and did not want to be helped. Without hesitation, Kelis gathered all her things and left.

As she was walking through the lobby of the building, she ran into Cruising. A look of surprise was painted on his face, but that look was indeed an act. He was Sasha's man, and everything she felt or feared, she confessed. Sitting at the desk was that retarded looking lobby security guard that always drooled whenever Kelis was around. There he was tongue and tail still wagging. Knowing just how smitten he was over her, she dropped her two duffle bags and kept walking. He just grabbed them and put them in his locker. Poor thing, he willingly took it and did not have a clue what could have been in it …another one bites the dust!

Standing in front of the condo waiting for car service, Bleu pulls up in a brand-new Mercedes Benz with his new girlfriend. So, not trying to stare, Kelis just waved her hand and looked the other way. As the valet takes his car, Bleu, and his new bitch, headed in her direction. She was praying that they would just keep walking, but they did not. Now, if not ever, was she in the mood for small pleasantries. Kelis was on a mission and even five minutes of her time, she couldn't spare. She had a little more than an hour and a half to get downtown to the pawn shop and to meet Smutty Low. Yes Smutty, you would think after their last encounter, she would have been done with him. In time, he would be dismissed, but right now, he knew where all the big games were. Although she felt uncomfortable around strangers, most of them were very familiar with her because of her family's reputation.

When Bleu approached her, his girlfriend continued walking like she should have. When he got up close, he reached out to touch her hands, but she quickly put them in her pocket. He asked how she had been lately, and she replied that she was fine. Then he asked, "Why haven't you ever called me?" She replied, "For what?" "Kelis, you know I love you and probably always will," he said. While he was spilling all his tea, her Uber arrived and she walked away from him, just like she did the pitiful lobby security guard. While she was walking away, he said to her that if she ever needed him, he was there. No words poured from her mouth and all that was heard was the closing of the cab door.

It took all of 30 minutes to get over the bridge to the pawn shop in Brooklyn. When she got inside, the line was long, but patiently she stood. Go figure, there was a time when Kelis had the patience of a bumble bee getting at some honey in a jar. No longer does she pant, complain, or raise eyebrows. Her addiction showed her who's boss and she was its best employee.

While standing in line, someone called out her name. As she looked around slowly, the face of the voice walked up to her. Oh, she was so ashamed to be there. She acted like she did not know the girl, but when the girl mentioned Bay Ridge High School, everything fell into place. Kelis was more than ashamed wearing shades and a wig proved it. She went to the pawn shop like someone would rob a bank. Turns out it was no other than Destiny. They were arch enemies in school, and one day, she and her bestie tried to jump Kelis in the school bathroom. Thanks to Sasha, shit was handled, and out of all the bitches in the world, she had to run into this girl in all places?

No matter the situation, Kelis always had a smart mouth, and that attitude was now heightened. That's when she said to Destiny, "Yes Bitch it's me." "Hey, Girl, how are you?" Destiny asked. Kelis responded by taking off her shades and wig, shook her hair around and said, "You be the judge." "Come on now, I know you're not still holding a grudge after all these years?" Destiny said. "Hell, yeah, and you better get the fuck out of my face before I give you more of that ass whipping that is owed to you," Kelis said. Destiny then quickly walked away and was probably thinking, wow, this girl is still crazy! Trust me, Kelis was no more bothered today than those days in high school. She used yesterday's issues to blow the girl off in the only way she knew she could.

The line shortened quickly, and she finally passed her jewelry under the cage window, along with her identification. Kelis's jewelry was valued at over 50 thousand dollars, except her father's ring given to her mother. She had it appraised years ago, but when you take jewelry to the pawn shop, you do not get merely what you pay for unless the gold is weighed heavily. She was not expecting its appraisal amount but something close in the ballpark. When the pawn shop employee offered her a mere 10 thousand dollars, she was floored. After they went back and forth, he demanded that she take it or leave it. So desperate and with no other alternative, Kelis gave the man all her jewelry, except her father's ring, which she vowed never to ever part with.

Leaving the pawn shop, she called Smutty, who was already coming out and about, and decided to meet Kelis on Jay Street. When they finally met up, he informed her that the game was canceled. It was still early in the day, but Kelis needed a fix immediately. Smutty made plenty of calls, but nothing was popping off at that moment. It was an early Wednesday afternoon, and instead of going home and chilling, Kelis decided to go to Atlantic City. Visiting there was something she had done a lot in her early 20s. Once you have thrown dice and cut cards in Monte Carlo, Rio de Janeiro, among many other exquisite places, AC looks like a one-arm bandit in the back of a bodega. Having to go back to where it all started is what some may say is coming full circle.

Truth be told, a gambler will gamble anywhere from the back of a street alley to the mountain tops of Switzerland. Also, they gamble with just about anyone who could match dollar for dollar. In no time, she and Smutty were filling his gas tank and riding down the turnpike. While on the road, Porsche called because Kelis was supposed to start work that day. Scheduling appointments for women to get silicone injections was not something Kelis ever wanted to do. Especially today when she thinks she has a way to make money. When she considered the job, she was desperate, but right now, she thinks she has a plan to go to AC to quadruple what she has in her pocketbook. As Porsche questions her, she gives her so many reasons and excuses. Her aunt knew she was riding high on what she thinks is a sure thing. As Kelis talks about herself, Porsche rudely interrupts her and tells her that she and her services would no longer be needed. Kelis laughed, hysterically, thinking her aunt's threats were a joke, but later found out she was nothing to play with. As soon as they got to Atlantic City, she immediately went to the poker table. Smutty took the time to get to their rooms and later caught up with her at the table. When he finally got situated and found Kelis, she was winning. She had doubled her money and was looking to get more. Smutty tried to convince her to take some time to chill, but she was thirsty. Three days later, reality hit, and she had lost everything, and he ended up leaving her once again. This time, he actually begged her to leave with him, but she was so determined to get her money back. It's been proven that people like Smutty are not typical gamblers. Those types know how to quit, especially when they're ahead. Unlike Kelis and many others, it's as hard as a mouse trying to flee a sticky pad, almost impossible.

She had one more day left to stay, she was as desperate as they came. She called everyone she thought cared, but none of her people were having it. Between calls, she walked the casino floors, looking everywhere but nowhere. Not so long ago, she could enter a room; men would drop their mouths, and a few bitches too. Either they were jealous or feeling her; nevertheless, they all looked with awe in their eyes. Kelis was still a sight, but that bright light had a few bulbs that had dimmed. It was now 10 o'clock and the last bus leaving AC was pulling out in 30 minutes. Kelis has never ridden the bus from AC back to New York, but this was not the time to be snotty but grateful. Surprisingly, a ticket was bought and left at the front desk from Smutty. Not in the rush to get on the bus, she decided to take the scenic route in hopes a miracle would happen. While walking through the casino, slow as possible, she ran into Big Mike. He was with a few friends, but when he saw her, he parted ways with them. The last time she and Mike were vibing, by night's end, they were at each other's throats. They had a disagreement over money, money she had not yet paid back. This time, in his presence, she is going to be a lot different, and he knows it. He knew she was strung out, and he finally had her just the way he intended.

P.S. ANYTHING YOU HAD NO BUSINESS INDULGING IN THE NIGHT PRIOR, THE MORNING AFTER IS GOING TO BE A MOTHER FUCKER! WHETHER IT'S GAMBLING MORE THAN YOU SHOULD OR WAKING UP NEXT TO SOMEONE ELSE'S MAN OR SOMEONE YOU DON'T EVEN KNOW. JUST REMEMBER TO ALWAYS OWN YOUR BEHAVIOR BECAUSE IT'S ONLY SO MUCH WE CAN BLAME BEING UNDER THE INFLUENCE FOR.

CHAPTER 32

THE MORNING AFTER

Just like it was once said and often written, never say, never. Kelis awakened and faced down between Big Mike's legs. She had no idea how she got to his hotel room but did not bother to question it. All she remembered was standing at the crap table, her hands on his bankroll while his hands were down her pants. As she looked around the room, there were plenty of half-opened bottles of champagne and Hennessey. If not for the semen on her face, leaky condoms on the bed, and the soreness of her pussy she wouldn't have believed it. Big Mike was not just a name given; it was given, justifiably so.

As she slowly tried to get his leg up from around her body, he would tighten more. It was like trying to get from under the wrath of a python. After trying so desperately to ease her way from underneath his legs, he finally loosened up and she was free. She was so eager to get the hell out of there. Finding her clothes was like trying to find a needle in a haystack. The hotel room was in such a mess, and she couldn't find anything but her underwear. After 10 more minutes, she finally found the rest of her clothing. Big Mike had hidden them on top of the closet. There was no need to wear dirty underwear, so she threw them in the garbage. Part of her mission was complete, and now it was time to clean her ass and break out.

While she was in the shower, Big Mike came into the bathroom. He went through her bag and noticed she had a couple of thousands of dollars tucked away between her small Bible. He then jumped in the shower, and she quickly jumped out. "Where are you going?" he asked. "I don't know, but I'm getting the fuck out of here," Kelis said. "Come on now, I am not done," he said. "Yes, the fuck you are," Kelis said. He then forcefully grabbed her by her hair and slammed her against the shower walls. He repeatedly did it until she finally gave up the fight. Last night, Kelis gave Big Mike plenty of pussy of free will, but today, here in that shower, Kelis was raped consistently and when he was not forcing his penis in her vagina, he was forcing it in her mouth. When it was all over, he had the audacity to act as if nothing had happened and even helped her get dressed. It was date rape at its finest, and just before he allowed her to leave, he lectured her about why he did what he did.

It was all payback for the many years she treated him and many others in the neighborhood like shit. For every word that was never said or thank you for many doors that were opened, he felt justified. She defended herself by telling him she never remembered him or intentionally tried to hurt him. Furthermore, the more she talked in her defense, the more pissed off he became. Whether she remembered him or not, he was still upset weeks ago at the card game and definitely last night at the craps table. Also, finding that two thousand dollars in her purse, she poured salt into the wound. So bad that he took an extra two grand out of her ass because when she ran into him, she was broken and bankrupt.

AC had bankrupted her, when he ran into her in the bus depot. In amazement, he wanted to know how she could have more money than him and he was the one that got her back in the game. She claimed that she had won, but since she started with nothing, she was not in a position to gain anything. Big Mike was still holding a grudge from the card game in Staten Island. He did everything he could to intimidate and physically hurt her, but what he did not know was that Kelis was a different kind of beast. She learned long ago how to channel her pain, and through the entire ordeal, her soul left the building. So, all that gibberish and pain he inflicted went unheard, and she became untouchable because she was then and had always been covered by GOD!

Finally, he was done preaching, and that is when she began to track star her way up out of there. Just before her hand touched the knob of the door, he noticed her father's ring on her finger. He joked about how she could pawn it and use the money for bus fare. She sarcastically told him that she would walk home from Atlantic City before she ever sold it. He said, "That's good because you wouldn't get five dollars for it, anyway." "This ring has sentimental value, and she wouldn't part with it for anything in the world," she said. He quickly replied, "Yeah, right Bitch, if I gave you $100 for it, you would be downstairs at either the poker table or slot machine." She looked at him as if she would, but a tear swelled in her eyes, and she headed for the door.

As much as she would've never considered parting with her father's ring, Big Mike hit a nerve and she was tempted. Her willingness to ignore his offer made him realize what the ring meant to her. He then grabbed her hand and aggressively took the ring off her finger. During the struggle, Kelis gave Big Mike a better fight than moments before, but he was a man and way too strong. She hysterically started crying and begged him to give it back. As she pleaded with him, she told him that the ring was given to her mother by her father. Big Mike laughed in her face, and it was obviously clear he did not give a fuck. Finally, someone had gotten to Kelis and all it took was a cheap ring that was probably worth no more than $50 but was priceless to her.

Moments later, she was sprawled out in front of his hotel room, hollering, and screaming. Many guests open their doors and close them thinking they were a couple having a domestic squabble. There are no concerns because that sought of behavior goes on in many hotels every day. Laying on the floor of the hotel, her battle scars were quite visual, but the ones that weren't noticeable were the daggers in her heart. Once she realized there was nothing she could do, she made a call to the one person she thought she never would need… Bleu. During that phone call, all he wanted to know was where she was. He then told her to go downstairs to the concierge. When she got downstairs, she was given a key to a luxurious suite. Kelis had hit rock bottom and calling Bleu made it official. She could have called Sasha, Suki, or her aunt Porsche, and they all would've at least made sure she had gotten home. For the first time in her life, Kelis was starting to own up to her addiction. Acknowledging you have a problem is the first step, but it takes more than just confessing, but doing something about it.

At that moment, Kelis felt defeated, lifeless, and extremely desperate, but desperation is an emotion that many addicts experience. She was indeed sick and tired of being sick and tired but that too is part of the dilemma. Kelis found herself alone in the world and thought she grew up under the microscope of many. She was deeply wounded and the only person who never hesitated to lick her wounds and apply a bandage was Bleu. He was a good man, and even a good man can become sick and tired. Kelis's journey was a troublesome one. She believed that she could avoid life's heartache by not falling in love. Love is beautiful, so beautiful that it is better to have loved than to never have it. That is why we should enjoy the process and not the work it took to get there.

PS. SHE LOVES ME... SHE LOVES ME NOT.

CHAPTER 33

STILL FEENING

As fast as lightning could appear across the sky, Bleu was faster to come to Kelis's rescue. When he finally got to the room, she was in a deep sleep and appeared totally out of it. Bleu took the liberty to order food, some personal things for her, and the hotel's finest champagne. As she slept, he hovered over her like a mama bear protecting her cub. Sometime later that night, Kelis finally awakened but was not in the mood Bleu imagined. So, in trying to keep the peace, he stood out of her way and allowed her to feel whatever she was feeling. He knew something had gone down here tonight but wouldn't go into any details until she was ready to talk about it.

For a moment, things got really ugly, but he wasn't unresponsive because he knew she was going through something much uglier. It was almost like a heroin addict detoxing; but unlike a heroin addict, she had no diarrhea or vomiting. Kelis was having an emotional detox and those are far worse than the physical ones. She was very angry, but most of her anger was well embedded in her long before she ever became addicted to gambling. Gambling released endorphins in her body that made her feel good. Endorphins are neurotransmitters released by the pituitary gland and hypothalamus in the brain. The body releases endorphins when you do pleasurable acts such as sex, exercise, and eating, but Kelis gets her endorphins when gambling. This breakdown was a long time coming, and finally, Kelis was coming to terms with real-life shit. She no longer lived in the land of make-believe.

Throughout the rest of the night, when she was done with the screaming and breaking shit, a sense of peace intervened. The worst was over, and I tell you, there's nothing like a man who knows how to remain cool under the worst circumstances. Especially when a woman is not having a good day. Room service had made its last trip and everything he thought she needed was delivered. He ordered her favorite meal and cocktail, along with beautiful dozens of white roses. Black orchids were her favorite flower, but if not for the late notice, her room would have been filled with them, as they were in Vegas. The silence was loud and if only it had a name. There was so much to discuss, but Bleu was a patient man. So, until she was ready to talk, he was not going to badger her.

Most of the night, Kelis sat in silence, but her face was extremely loud. After much observing, Bleu rolled himself a blunt and then went into the bathroom to take a shower. After a hot splash, another blunt rolled, then off to bed, he went. The day was long, but tomorrow was going to be longer and very controversial. It was the calm before the storm and as he gestured to hug her before saying goodnight; she neglected to reciprocate. Being the kind of man that he was, he did not dissect the behavior. He let it roll off his shoulders while he rolled up in the covers.

Five minutes in the dark, the sound of whimpering came from beneath the sheets. Considering what mood she was in, Bleu had no idea how to approach the matter, so he laid still and did nothing. She was swallowed by emotion when she reached for him. Finally, the kind of reaction Bleu was hoping for. Their bodies were entwined so close they appeared as one. Their passion for one another has always been so intense, so intense to deny. Bleu has always been honest about his feelings, while Kelis has always played hardball. Protecting her heart was something she had to learn to do. How many times can a heart be shattered into a million pieces? Love is not just a feeling; it is an act made from an emotion. Many are ecstatic to find it in a lifetime, while some believe they could do without it. Kelis was among that group. The temperature of her body combined with his could set off the smoke alarm. Tears rolled down her face as he kissed them dry. When morning came, they both were in a different mindset. Kelis was indeed much happier than a day ago but would be happier if she could go downstairs.

Twenty-four hours had passed, and it was now time for Kelis to tell him the truth and nothing but. Bleu sat on a chair across from the bed while Kelis sat opposite. Kelis knew he wanted the whole truth and while she did not want to talk about it, she knew she had to. So, she started from the beginning but tried to leave a lot of the story out. Bleu knew parts of her story made no sense, so he remained patient and warned her to tell it like it was and not what she wanted it to be. Still playing games and ignoring his wants, she continued telling her side but left much of the story in the dark. That's when Bleu became enraged and grabbed her. He did not grab her to hurt her but to shake her up a bit. However, the rage she had for Big Mike was amplified and Bleu was now the enemy in the room. In order to get her to stop attacking him, he had to slap her hard.

Seems like when he did, something shifted, and all her aggression softened. She then fell to the floor and revealed everything. She told Bleu that she went up to Big Mike's room to fuck him in exchange for some monetary favors. When morning came, while in the shower, he found money in her bag. That made him furious, so furious he raped her. "How could you say he raped you? Didn't you just tell me that you came to his room to fuck him in exchange for some money he gave you?" Bleu asked. "Yes, I gave him some pussy, as a matter of fact, plenty, but the next day, he took advantage of me and also took my father's ring. He knew he couldn't break me but taking my father's ring, he did," Kelis said.

Throughout her confession to Bleu, she broke down and fell into his arms. He then quickly grabbed his phone, but Kelis begged him not to call on a hit. The reason is Big Mike once worked for Bleu when he was 14 years old. He knew too much about him and it would be almost suicide for him to retaliate. Bleu was a man that was not afraid of anything and was not worried about some small-time motherfucker he once took under his wing. Although Bleu had no concerns, Kelis knew better. The streets are different for her and also for Bleu. The bad guys are much younger, toddlers to be exact. They are unimaginably notorious and would kill you just because they could.

After hours of begging Bleu to calm down, he finally did. The rest of the morning was hot chocolate and strawberry short cake, Kelis's favorite. There was a little bit of champagne still in the bottle and a half of blunt to smoke. After a long day finally, they both became exhausted and called it an early night. It was about 10 o'clock when Bleu called downstairs for an early morning checkout. He lay down besides, Kelis thinking they both were on the same path. Unfortunately, she was willing to drive in the same car but needed to go down her own road. The road is called the road of destruction. That road that leads to nowhere but has plenty of detours, slippery roads, and a would-be sign that should warn you that the bridge is out.

P.S. JUST YESTERDAY, SHE HIT ROCK BOTTOM, BUT SHE WAS NOT DONE FEEDING HER ADDICTION UNTIL THE DISEASE WAS DONE WITH HER.

CHAPTER 34

PAYBACK IS A MOTHER FUCKER!

Revenge is sometimes more deadly to the one looking to get payback than its target. When Kelis confessed to Bleu about her ordeal, he never got over it. Although he appeared reasoned that infamous poker face, he convinced her differently. Once again, the student became better at reading and writing than the teacher. When he awakened, she was gone and every dime in his pocket was too. That's when he knew her problem was far more serious than he was willing to admit. He quickly called downstairs to the casino; his spies informed him that Kelis was seated gambling at a poker table. He demanded they keep an eye on her and in about five minutes, Bleu was dressed and headed downstairs.

When he got there, she was intoxicated, mixing Hennessey with orange juice. She was unexpectedly winning, something these days she finds hard to do. For a while, he just observed the game, but when she had won a pot for five thousand dollars, he walked up alongside her and told her to get up. What Bleu quickly learned, a gambler does not know when to get up, especially when they're winning. Getting Kelis up from that table was like taking a bone from a hungry dog and that wasn't going to happen. The difference here is that Bleu was not playing games with her anymore, and that sweet man who loved her unconditionally was now protecting his own heart. All that he had given her, she was now in a place where she was stealing and showing him no respect. Furthermore, he thought she was on a path to change and then he realized there wasn't anything more he could do for her. When she refused to get up, he grabbed her and picked her up over his shoulders.

It was early in the morning and not that many people were downstairs yet. Seated around the table were three men, a lady, and two dealers. Kelis felt that since she was in the hotel, she would be protected, so she decided to really perform. She then began to holler and scream, but Bleu was well known and liked by many of the hotel security. Who would have ever thought, even in Atlantic City, that he was the man? On their way to the elevator, guess who walks out with three of his goonies... Big Mike. Bleu had Kelis over his shoulders when Big Mike passed, chuckling. He then shouted out, "Everything you ever had, I got... even your bitch!" Kelis knew where this was about to go, so now, instead of Bleu holding on to her, she was holding on to him. Just when the elevator door opened, Bleu threw her into it and told her to go back to the room and remain there. This time, Kelis saw fire in his eyes and knew there was nothing she could do but pray and hope he would make it back upstairs in one piece.

Bleu was a man on a mission and this matter had to be settled for so many reasons. First of all, why rape a woman, especially when she has already given you enough pussy to last a lifetime? Secondly, what man calls another man's woman a bitch to his face? Last but not least, this same little boy once lived on the streets and was physically abused by family members. Bleu took him in and took good care of him. Bleu wanted more for him since he, too, was a product of a broken home. Big Mike chose the same path as Bleu, and that is something Bleu will not beat himself up about. The many reasons on this topic could go on and on, but Bleu was done with reasonings and whys.

When he finally caught up to Big Mike, it was business from start to finish. It got so bad that Big Mike's groupies made no attempt to get into the ring with Bleu, so there were now four bitches in the room. Bleu whipped his ass so badly that the negro began to holler for forgiveness. During his beatdown, he also started screaming for help, but security muttered to keep the noise down while looking the other way. Just when Bleu was about done emasculating Big Mike, he reminded him about the days he once cared for him as a daddy but now had to kick his ass like his father!

When Bleu finally made it back to the room, he was bloodied and a little bruised. Kelis was so concerned about his well-being and tried to tend to his wounds. Seems like her bedside manner was not needed and the way he was maneuvering, she felt it too. For the first time, the only man outside of her father who loved her throughout was done with her. No pussy, no blow job, or pretty face could have convinced him to stay. Just when he was walking out of the door, she then started confessing her feelings, something he wanted to hear so long ago. It was almost like a "Gone with the Wind" moment… He quickly said, "Frankly, Kelis, I DON'T GIVE A DAMN!" As he closed the door behind him. She wiped her tears, changed her clothes, and went back downstairs.

For the next three days, she gambled all her money away until she was completely broke. The ride home from AC was quick, and instead of going to Brooklyn, she took the train to Randalls Island. There at Randalls Island was Gambler's Anonymous. She ran across the brochure a long time ago and never forgotten its address. When she arrived, she paced in front of the building for about an hour before walking in. When she finally got the nerve to walk in, she took a seat in the back of the room. After listening to many of the people in the room's confessions, she realized that she was just as fucked up. What started as a drive-by ended up as a three-hour encounter. When it was all over, she was asked to be given a sponsor, but she was still in the beginning stages and was still in a bit of denial. A sponsor is someone you can call or relate to when needed. They are there for your good and bad days and could be so instrumental to those who feel like they are alone. Addiction could be a lonely place, considering people, places, and things are their triggers.

Leaving the meeting that night, she had no place to go. If necessary, she could go back to family or friends, but she didn't want to burden anyone anymore. If she was going to get better, she was going to do it solely on her own. She did have one ace up her sleeve and that was going to Ms. Remsen. Long ago, Ms. Remsen's granddaughter came into their lives and stole Porsche man away from her. Not only did he walk away from Porsche, but he also married the bitch, and they had a baby. Therefore, that was a long time ago, and time has healed old wounds, and everyone is happy living their own lives. Honestly, Ms. Remsen shouldn't have been put in the middle of their bullshit, and hopefully, she won't be carrying a grudge. When Kelis got to Ms. Remsen's house, it was like old times. People were everywhere, drinking, gambling, and partying. The house was so disgusting, filled with Negros and garbage cans overflowing with dirty pampers. Ms. Remsen was one foot on a banana peel and one in the grave, but she was still Ms. Remsen talking shit and could not stomp a grape. She was glad to see Kelis; unfortunately, it was from the last eye that still worked. After an hour had gone by, Kelis became tempted by her surroundings, and was out of there. Ms. Remsen's home was filthy, filled with not just germs but also her ungrateful, nasty granddaughters. How could three grown women share a home and don't clean the fucking toilet? It's almost impossible to keep your ass clean and not your bathroom. That's like daily stepping out of the shower into the sewer. A clean ass is kept at its finest when supported by a fairly clean environment.

Suddenly, Kelis received a phone call on her way to leaving Ms. Remsen's home. It was a Porsche; she was locked up. She was set up by a transgender named Honeybee. He had been coming to get injections for years, and somehow, he had caught a bad infection. Porsche had explained to him and all her clientele how to take care of themselves outside of the clinic. It was later revealed the Honeybee had gotten injections out of the state but figured it was easier to blame Porsche's expertise. How things went from a dissatisfied customer to her behind bars is something we'll probably never know. However, she is now locked up and in a lot of trouble. Moving her place of business was not a good idea, but now is not the time to second guess any bad choices. Porsche had one phone call and needed Kelis to get her a lawyer. Lawyers are needed, and money is, too, when you're in this kind of trouble. She had confided in Kelis about some money she had hidden in her Queens apartment. Secretly hiding money is something she learned from her mother. Thank goodness for that because all her bank accounts were frozen, and if not for mad money, she wouldn't have been able to pay her bail. When her aunt offered her the job, for many reasons, going to jail was Kelis's biggest issue because she suffered from claustrophobia or being around nothing, but women would have immediately killed her. During their conversation, Kelis was on the verge of saying I told you so, but never would she kick her aunt while she was down.

Once she got to her aunt's apartment, a key was given to her by the doorman. Surprisingly, that was put in place a long time ago. The apartment was eerie, and it reminded her of walking into her grandmother's house after it was vacant. Memories were smeared over the walls like paint. You could visualize life that once moved through the rooms. After a long hot shower, she nestled on the couch with a glass of wine. Everything about today was beginning to fade away. Tomorrow's another day and if we pray, hopefully we will be lucky enough to see it!

P.S. MOST TIMES, WE ARE PUT THROUGH ROUGH WATERS BECAUSE OUR ENEMIES CANNOT SWIM.

CHAPTER 35

MIDNIGHT TRAIN TO GEORGIA

It was 6 a.m., and Kelis was still laid out across her aunt's sofa. She was leaving to post bail this morning but was so tempted to call Smutty Low and see what game may be popping off today. She had found 100 thousand dollars in her aunt's apartment, hidden everywhere. Her aunt had hidden money in the fridge, under mattresses and behind toilets. Her bail was 50 thousand dollars, so, in her mind, she was good, and so would her auntie.

The devil is a mother fucker and her desire to gamble was intense. After hours of praying and pacing the floor, yesterday's meeting was still fresh in her memory, but today, the temptation was beating the hell out of it. After spending most of the morning struggling to do right, she finally made a call to Suki. Calling him to handle her aunt's affairs has proven the devil had once again won. Suki was the type of friend who could not hold a grudge or stay mad at you no matter what you did. Unlike Sasha, she was a lot like Kelis and that is why they dealt with one another so differently. When Kelis called him for help, he tried to ignore her sirens, but he loved her and dived in to help without question. When he showed up at the apartment, he was looking better than he had ever and was in a gossiping mood. Normally, Kelis is not in the who's zooming, who mood, but it's been a while since she has entertained Suki's soap opera moments. After Suki dished the tea, about others, he saved the best tea for last…. Bleu. He told Kelis that Bleu had stopped by his apartment to say goodbye to him and Blaze. He told them that he was moving to Atlanta, Georgia. He expressed no particular reason for leaving but did say there was nothing left for him in Brooklyn. All Kelis could do was stand still for a second, then move around the topic as if Suki hadn't said a word. Suki was also outspoken and for many years, Kelis's relationship with Bleu was untouchable until today. Suki, coming to the aid of Kelis this morning, had its own agenda. He came here to tell her that the best thing that ever happened to her was about to leave town. He also admitted that he and everyone had known how fucked up she had been and that it was time for her to come out of the cold. Still in pain and still highly self-medicating, she thanked him for coming and escorted him out of the door. Before leaving, he invites her to come to Jada's 10th birthday party. "Wow, 10 years old; where did the time go?" Kelis said. As the door opens, he looks back and says, "Yeah, children aren't the only ones that get old and grow up."

Later that evening, her aunt's bail was paid, and she was free. By this time, she had called an Uber and was on her way to meet Smutty Low. She had taken five thousand dollars and left the rest of her aunt's money where she could find it in the fridge. Jada's party was beginning at three o'clock, and yet she was heading to meet up with Smutty around 2:30. Sometimes in life with prayer, some things happen when you least expect and without much effort. Somewhere between Queens and heading to the Bronx, Kelis ended up in Brooklyn. When they say "JESUS," take the wheel, He truly does. There she was, sitting in an Uber parked across the street from her old house. She was struggling and afraid and did not know how she got there, but she was so glad she was. Going back to where it all started was like going forward. The Uber driver was patient, but after some time, he informed her that her time was up and he had to move on. She replied that she needed some more time and that he would be accommodated excessively. While she was deciding her next move, she got a call, but it was the wrong number. Ironically, the number was exactly her grandmother's old house phone number with a different area code. That was so spooky, like her grandmother was calling her from the grave. The day had already started with its uncertainty and now this! Suddenly again, a second call came, and it was Smutty and just when she decided to grace him with her presence, she got a call from Jada. She had called to see if Kelis was coming to her birthday party. Not wanting to break her godchild's heart, she quickly said yes and that she was on her way. Her date with the devil was indeed going to happen, but first, she had a date with an angel.

When the Uber pulled up to Suki's Brooklyn Heights brownstone apartment, Black Barbies were aligned up the steps. The dolls were dressed in hot pink and so were Jada and Suki. The party was a Barbie theme and Blaze was dressed up as Ken. I tell you; Suki loves the dramatics of these types of things, and it was hard to know which birthday party it was. Suki pulled out all the stops, and the party had everything but other children attending. Over the years, he has gotten better at parenting but needs to understand that he cannot be everything to his children. Children need peers of their own to bond with and it doesn't matter what level you can relate to them on. That is a subject Kelis knew too well.

However, the party was over the top, fabulous and had Suki's name all over it. It's been some time since Kelis had bonded with the children, and she did not know just how much she missed the love. While in Jayden's room, the doorbell rang. The Dalmatians started barking really loud and when they wouldn't stop, Kelis made it her business to see what the commotion was all about. It was Sasha and Cruising and what looked like a 5-year-old child in her stomach. It never crossed her mind to find out about her friend's pregnancy results after leaving her in the bathroom that day sick as a dog. Not only was she pregnant, but she also looked like she was about to have a litter of puppies.

No shade: her friend was enormous, happy, and very much in Love. When they locked eyes, the last six months meant nothing, and they both embraced and went on as if nothing had happened. That's the luxury of having a real friend. You both can get really frustrated with each other's shit, but you don't let it break the friendship, especially because you both are not on the same page. Being in the apartment with her friends, breaking bread and sipping brew was like old times, and for the most part, at the moment, Kelis was content. Occasionally, during the evening, she made attempts to leave, but whenever she did, the children and her two friends prevented her from doing so. Also, what she had always envisioned was occurring and that put shackles around her ankles. It was Sasha and Suki with their significant others spending time together and no one feeling uncomfortable. There was a time when that was impossible, but to see them all genuinely happy was so beautiful. The room was filled with nothing but love, and although Kelis was there alone, her God children were giving her that good old unconditional love. The kind of love only innocent children could provide.

It was going on 9 o'clock, and the children had been bathed and put to bed. The grown folks were now having to entertain themselves and that was the best part of the party. Sasha was about to fall asleep, while Cruising was massaging her feet. Suki was going around collecting dirty cups and plates, trying to get his place back the way he liked. Once again, unexpectedly, the doorbell rang, and this time, not only were the dogs startled, but everyone in the apartment. Quickly, Cruising reached for his gun while Suki came out of the kitchen with a machete in his hand. Where we come from, nobody comes to anyone's house after 6 pm without notice.

Nonetheless, they all were on point, but when the door opened, all mouths were wide. It was Bleu and he did not look like he was there to partake in the festivities. He was on his way, leaving town and wanted to drop something off to Blaze. Naturally, he was invited in, and then he and Blaze went into the other room to talk. While they were holding court in the next room, Kelis decided now, if any, was it the best time for her to go. Somehow, her coat went missing, and while they all went on a scavenger hunt to look for it, she was held captive until it was discovered. Suddenly, Bleu and Blaze emerged from the room, and so did everyone else.

Somehow, the partygoers caught a second wind, and Suki was back playing music and pouring drinks. That is when it dawned on Kelis that this was a setup. Not only were they all in cohorts, but Bleu was also caught off guard. By now, she was ready to leave without a coat and he was looking like he just wanted to be gone. As Kelis stood in the middle of Suki's apartment, refusing to sit down, Sasha and Suki to refuge in front of the door. Initially Bleu appeared angry, but after a few pulls on a blunt, his mood had changed. One thing Kelis knew was that leaving that apartment was not going to be easy, but she knew they could not hold her captive forever. An hour had passed, and we all were seated together quietly. Sasha and Cruising were practically so close; any closer, she would've given birth. Suki was seated between Blaze's legs, the only place on earth he would rather be. Bleu was seated to the left of the lovebirds, while Kelis was seated at the dining room table. Blaze had a serious jazz collection being played most of the night, and it was suddenly interrupted by some good R&B music. Just when Kelis thought the night was a bust, the right song came on and put her in another time and place. Whatever she was feeling, obviously, it boomeranged because Bleu was feeling it, too. It was a well-thought-out plan, and only those close to her knew how to pull something like this off. She was still playing hardball and that pissed Sasha the fuck off. So, she abruptly pulled Kelis into the bathroom. Sasha was like EF Hutton; when she spoke, Kelis knew to listen. When they got into the bathroom, she told Kelis to not only sit the fuck down but the shut the hell up! She went A to Z. When she was done, all Kelis could do was walk out of the bathroom, and all that sass was put on pause.

CHAPTER 36

TRAIN DERAILED

Whatever Sasha said, Kelis came out of that bathroom a different woman, and Bleu was here for it. For the moment, neither of them said much, but their body temperament spoke volumes. Since most of the food that Suki had prepared earlier was eaten, more food was ordered and delivered. When the delivery man came through the door, he was accompanied by an extra bundle of goodies, Porsche. Her timing was on point and her visit was way overdue. Previously that day, she had been bailed out and was told that Kelis was there visiting. When she entered Suki's apartment, she thanked him for taking the time to post her bail, but she desperately needed to talk to her niece. So afraid of what Porsche would say in front of everyone, Kelis hurried to talk to her in the next room. Surprisingly, her aunt was there to say goodbye. She had decided to leave Brooklyn and start over in Chicago. In Chicago was Lexus and since getting married, she had given birth to three babies in the last two years. Chicago was going to be a fresh start and being able to help Lexus raise her children was going to be so fulfilling. Porsche always loved children but, unfortunately, because of a botched abortion, was unable to have any. Coming to check on Kelis was last on her to-do list before heading to her apartment. Her flight to Chicago was leaving early in the morning and she knew she could not leave without saying goodbye. There were so many things she wanted to say to Kelis, but she did not want to get things heated and leave on bad terms. Without hesitation, she told her to take good care of herself and that she loved her. As Porsche walked to the door, Kelis dug in her pocketbook and handed Porsche an envelope. In that envelope was the five thousand dollars she had stolen from her aunt's stash. When Kelis reached out to put the money in Porsche's hand, she grabbed her tightly. Porsche had already been to her apartment and knew Kelis had stolen the money. She only went to look for Kelis, hoping she would be honest enough to return it. When Kelis willingly returned the money, both of their eyes swelled with tears. Never did Porsche want to believe that her Niece would have stolen from her, but if she had, the love would have still been there, along with disappointment. Porsche's job there was done, and she put the money back in Kelis's hand, but before Kelis could accept it, Bleu said, "Thank you but no thank you." He then folded the envelope more securely and handed it back to Porsche. That's when Porsche said, "Girl, you better hold on to this guy; he is for sure a keeper." She then pulled them both towards her, kissed them both on the forehead and bid them goodbye. Walking out the door, she asked Suki to play her favorite song, dedicated to her favorite couple…. "You Know How to Love Me" by the late great Phyllis Hyman!

As the song played over and over, Kelis sang along, dedicating every word to him. When they weren't dancing, they were embracing, and their love was advertised for the world to see. It was obviously clear the spell had broken, and she was now under new construction. They were so wrapped up in each other's world that they lost sight of who, what, where, and why. Nevertheless, their friends would sleep out in the cold in exchange for their happiness. When they finally came up for air, the room was empty and quiet, and that conversation that needed to be had begun. Anything that was going to be said would not be held against anyone and now was the time to speak or forever hold their peace. Since Bleu was the one with not much to confess, he went first. He told Kelis that he apologized for trying to control her. He explained that since he has never come to terms with his mother's death, he viewed her in Kelis's eyes. Also, when they were together, especially in the beginning, every argument, time apart, or minor breakup triggered that pain and it felt like another loss. Although it was two different scenarios and people involved, the pain hit home all the same. Having to work through their breakup this last time around brought closure. It helped him understand that it is OK for a man to show as much love as he wants towards his woman. Just as long as she does not feel like she is in bondage while enduring it. Learning to understand Kelis's pain had so much to do with him owning his own. His confession was short but so meaningful because, at the end of the day, all a woman wants is to be heard and understood! It is usually to save the best for last, but in this case, it was the worst. Before she got started, she reached in a kissed him. He could tell she was nervous, but it was he who was just as anxious.

Not knowing where to begin, she followed her heart and let the words pour from it and out her mouth. There was no going back to the many loves lost she endured since birth. Bleu, of all people, knew her story, and that is why she was always frustrated with his behavior. She started off by saying how much she loved him and why it was so hard for her to acknowledge it. While growing up, she watched her mother's love for a man devour her. Nevertheless, her mother was a young girl, smitten by her first love, and tragically, he killed himself. Kelis knew her father's death had to be devastating for her mother, but when her father took his life, he took way too many others with him. The day he died, so did her mother, his mother, and, in many other ways, her grandmother. It was a domino effect and Kelis was the last peg to fall. Halfway through her story, she let him know that she would not be talking about the men in her past and neither did he need to talk about all those bitches he fucked. She was not one to kiss and tell and if so, she was not going to jeopardize their reunion by naming names. Now it was time to address the obvious… the gambling. Before diving in, let's all take a deep breath… she said she could sit here and blame her addiction on the many loved ones lost or because the sun didn't shine today. Truth be told, she loved partying, hanging out, and a good shot of brandy. Way before it ever became addictive, at the tender age of six, she would sneak down to her grandmother's basement just to get a glimpse of people having a good old time. She was drawn in by the shuffling of cards and Motown recordings that serenaded her to sleep. Although her bedroom was located on the second floor, the smell of nicotine and alcohol also became her roommate. With all she had to endure, it's a wonder gambling was the only thing she could not control.

After many more hours of confessions and analyzing her problems, the only question left was, what was she prepared to do about it? She had many options, but Bleu was only concerned about the one that led her back to him. He was no longer in the business of controlling or manipulating her; he wanted her to make the best choice for herself, and if that meant her walking away from him again, he was willing to accept it. He then got his coat and told her that he'd be leaving by midnight on the train to Atlanta, Georgia. "Why the train and why Atlanta?" she asked. Trains have always been something he loved as a kid. The few times he has ever road the train as a child with his mom was the best adventure ever. When he started making money in the streets, it was all about jetting around on private planes and taking the train was a poor man's choice. He was now living his life according to his wants and did not care what the naysayers were talking about. Also, Atlanta is where his mother originated and recently, he has gotten in touch with a few distant cousins there. Talks of family and how much she missed the love and dynamics had him yearning to put down some roots. Before he walked out the door, he looked back and blew her a kiss. He then said, "I'll be going back to my apartment to gather the rest of his things, so if this is goodbye, take care and if it is not, let's go!"

As much as she wanted to take his hand, she couldn't. She was still afraid, and fear could stop you from learning, living, and loving. But fear was also something Bleu was feeling, but he was more afraid of not loving than love itself. Suddenly, the door closed, and everything around her went dark. It was like her life flashed in front of her and all she saw was that same little lost girl, afraid to love because of all the love she had lost. Sasha and Suki had entered the room to lick her wounds or whatever else she needed. They have always liked Bleu, but they were team Kelis always and forever. Neither of them said a word, but when she was ready to talk, that is when they would. Whenever any of them were having a bad day and broken up by something, a good old-fashioned cry followed by some good old school music and straight Henny, sometimes right out of the fucking bottle. Suki was having problems getting his music to start and when it did, the first song played was Gladys Knight, "Midnight Train to Georgia." The melody chimed in, but it was the lyrics that had Kelis running out of the door.

She didn't even take the time to grab her coat; thank goodness she had her pocketbook, or she would've left that too. It was a very cold night, but the love of her man was keeping her warm. Once she got about seven blocks from Suki's apartment, that's when she realized a car service was needed. So anxious to get to him, she reached into her bag to call him, but her phone and wallet were left on Suki's table. All that was in her bag was some toiletries, a bag of mini-Chips Ahoy cookies, and a small Bible. Time was of the essence, so she decided to hop on the train. With no money in her possession, going through the turnstile was her only option. As for as many times that has been done, of all days, she got caught. Luckily, after explaining her situation, the officer let her go. Kelis had a gift for gab, something she inherited from her grandmother and being fine as hell, something she inherited from her father, didn't hurt.

It took an hour and some change to get to Yonkers, but when she finally got there, she was freezing and wheezing. When she got to his block, she noticed his car parked on the corner, so she started walking toward his building. As she was walking, she noticed those bowed legs coming in her direction. Once he got up close, he was surprised to see her and so extremely happy. The first thing he did was hold her close and look her in the eyes. Then he said, "Are you ready to give up everything here and follow me?" At first, she couldn't speak, but then suddenly, she shook her head yes and hollered up to God for allowing her to come to a place where she could trust and not be afraid anymore.

He then immediately got to his car and ushered her in from the cold. After the ignition ran for a while, Kelis was warm. Once the car started purring like a satisfied woman, he jumped out. He said that he had forgotten one last thing and had to go back to his apartment to get it. She told him to leave whatever was there behind because all that he needed was already in the car. He laughed and agreed but told her that she would not be disappointed with what he was going back to retrieve. Before walking away, she had a bad premonition but allowed her faith in God to ignore it. Therefore, what appeared as a goodbye kiss was truly one. So, to keep the faith, she sat back in the car and tried to concentrate on what was ahead and what was not long ago. Bleu's apartment was just down the block, and going there should have only taken no more than 15 minutes, coming and going combined.

After another 20 minutes had passed, she decided to look for him. Getting out of his warm car after her body had just gotten the right temperature was a reaction of a terribly worried woman. As soon as she opened the door, she felt the iciness of the weather and started running quickly to his building. It was indeed very cold, but this time, the shivers were mostly brought by a terrible gut feeling in her stomach. When she got closer to his building, she was met by a horrific scream and that made her run faster. Once she got inside, he was slumped face down in front of his door. When she tried to turn him around, her hands were soaked with blood. Turns out he was shot in the back of his head twice. Each hole was visible and streaming an excessive amount of blood. By this time, she began to scream and that is when everyone in his building came out of their apartment. The mere sight of him caused panic amongst the neighbors and Kelis had to holler to someone to call the ambulance. While she was waiting for the EMS to arrive, she realized that the premonition had come true.

Suddenly after what seemed like a lifetime, the paramedic and police arrived. By that time, she was in shock, and they had to literally tear him from her arms. Bleu had a next-door neighbor named Ms. Colleen. She was like a mother to him and did her best to console Kelis. Once the paramedics declared him dead, his body remained on the hallway floor for hours. There is only one coroner in each borough, and oh boy, sometimes it seems like there's one for the entire state. While waiting for his body to be picked up, Kelis remained in Ms. Collen's home. She had a teenage granddaughter who wore the same size as Kelis, and since her clothes were soaked in blood, she was given some of her clothes, especially a jacket.

Eventually, the coroners arrived, and when his body was placed in the van, she broke down once again. Placing Bleu in that van was the same visual she experienced when her mother died. After she had given the proper information about Bleu, she walked down the block and sat in his car. While there, she had another emotional meltdown but somehow got things under control. Once she gained some composure, she called her two besties. They were devastated by the news and begged her to stay where she was because they were on their way. Fortunately, she was not going anywhere because she was bombarded with grief. Although Kelis was numb to loss, many have said that when a person loses a lover, they truly lose part of their being. Outside of her father, Kelis has never been in love with any man. Bleu was her first and she vowed that he would be her last.

P.S. THEY SAY IT IS GOOD TO HAVE BEEN LOVED THAN TO NOT HAVE BEEN LOVED AT ALL!

CHAPTER 37

NEVER SAY GOODBYE, BUT SEE YOU LATER

I t had been a year since Bleu's death and during that time, Kelis had gone away for treatment. It was not the typical rehab for substance abusers but more like a spiritual retreat. It was located in the Poconos, and twice a week out of the compound, she sought counseling for her gambling addiction. Kelis needed to get far away and come to terms with shit brewing from the time she was a small child to the woman she was today. Life on her farm was hard and there were no hens or chicken Coco dolling.

Bleu's murderer (Big Mike) was never apprehended, but Kelis and everyone on the streets knew he was the culprit. Life has a way of revenging on its own, then about three months later, Big Mike was also killed. He was found parked in his car with three bullets to his head. A note was found stuffed in his mouth that read, **NEVER BITE THE HAND THAT FEED YOU, BECAUSE THAT SAME HAND MAY BE THE ONE THAT KILLS YOU!**

When Bleu's personal things were given to her, she noticed, with his belongings, her father's ring. She never knew that Bleu had gotten the ring back and that is why he was determined to go back to the apartment that night. Bleu going back to his apartment for that ring was something Kelis would have always blamed herself for. Thank goodness for the help of good counselors and treatment; she would not have been able to forgive herself but pray that somewhere in Heaven, he was. Along with some day-to-day struggles, the day he kissed her and walked away runs through her mind consistently. That is why it is so important to always, before leaving a loved one, try to never leave each other on bad terms and always plant a kiss and "NEVER SAY GOODBYE, BUT SEE YOU LATER."

Kelis was an intelligent girl but allowed certain temptations to interfere with what she knew was good for her. She got caught up in a life upon which only she knew and got too comfortable. We all believe what's good to us is good for us, and much of that is a fact. But unfortunately, the things that give us the most pleasure are the things that are so detrimental. Once she learned why certain things made her click, she channeled it. Channeling something is also like mastering it. The better you learn to understand something, the better you become at dealing with it. There are so many reasons why many people obsessively indulge in things. Some say if you eat too much, you're greedy, or if you drink too much, you're an alcoholic. Truth be told, some obsessions are related to impulsive behaviors, but a lot of times, people just want to escape. Unfortunately, some of us don't ever want to get off the merry-go-round. Whatever your choice of illusion is, eating, drinking, shopping, sex, gambling, or drugs, there's never any escaping. Even during the moment of highly indulging, there's a part of your brain that will never get numb. That's why the average addict never gets enough. They will continue to try to climb that mountain but are eventually thrown off the cliff. Kelis was always aware of her addiction because where she came from, gambling was the norm and cool as a fuck. Playing cards was how her people enjoyed themselves on the weekends and sometimes during the week. Many of us don't have a rich uncle on life support, only what we bring home from our 9 to 5. Most times, what you bring home isn't enough so that you may need a side hustle. Making money on the side is brilliant and cool, just as long as it doesn't have you someday doing time.

However, card games were also a way to interact with associates, along with making a few coins. It's crazy how many who come to these games believe they have somewhere else better to be. If so, why show up, or better yet why are they there every freaking weekend? Kelis was raised and introduced to this life, like many who will read this book and will agree that playing cards isn't just a gambling thing; it's a BLACK THING! White people are known to play bridge, while Black people are known to play Pity Pat. There are other games of card, like Spades, Big Whisk, and Poker, but Pity Pat is the game of all games. Going to "Gambler's Anonymous was so good for her in so many ways, but having to dislocate herself from people, places, and things was the hardest.

Once she returned to Brooklyn after taking some time getting herself together, she got bored. Boredom is not good for anyone, especially an addict. The devil's workshop is at its busiest when an individual has nothing on their mind. Once she got home, Sasha had a four-month-old baby girl that she named after Kelis's mother. Her name was Mercedes Nicole, born on May 24, weighing 9lbs 6 oz. Her weight was clearly not a surprise, considering how big Sasha was carrying her.

Sasha and Cruising had gotten married just before her daughter was born. They exchanged vows at City Hall and the only ones in attendance were the two of them. Sasha's father had recently died, and her mother was going to live with her in Connecticut to help her raise the baby. Suki was still Suki and was trying to still get a handle on fatherhood. Jada and Jade were growing up so fast, and Suki found that to be so delightful, but sad.

He wants them to grow but still remain his babies. Of course, that is what every parent desires, but he really wants them to continue wearing onesies to bed. That shit makes no damn sense, but so does Suki.

When Sasha left for Connecticut, she allowed Suki to live in the Condo with his family. Once her father died, most of his property was sold, but Sasha refused to let go of the Condo since it was once home to us all and always will be. While visiting Sasha, she gave Kelis a box that contained Bleu's ashes. When she was away, she had given Sasha's address for his ashes to be sent there. Holding onto the box, she felt some anxiety, but after a while, a sense of peace covered her. Since Bleu's passing, she felt him near, but holding onto his ashes was quite surreal.

Two months had passed and after much consideration, Kelis decided it was time to move on. Leaving Brooklyn this time was going to be really hard because, unlike before, deep down inside, she knew she would return. But this time around, she's leaving with no initial plans of returning anytime soon, if ever. She had decided to go to Chicago for a while to be with her aunts, not necessarily to stay but to go before she made her final decision on what she wanted to do with her life. Kelis was now 37 years old and still beautiful, but that was no longer her main objective. She was on the road to healing and no longer concealing herself or her feelings. She was finally able to look at herself in the mirror and look past her beautiful skin tone and features and see her flaws and be OK with them.

The day she left for Brooklyn, she was supposed to go by Sasha's and Suki's place but instead decided to bid farewell on a three-way call. She sat in an Uber across the street from her old residence. A neighbor who lived on the block continued to get mail for her from the new owners of the house.

Most times, it was usually junk mail, but this time, a neatly sealed envelope was amongst the mail. While on the phone, she and her friends laughed and cried, but after exchanging such pleasantries, the conversation ended. No goodbyes were said, only see you later! She then sat back and viewed the block for one last time. Not much of the block had an effect on her, but those steps to her grandmother's house were once her throne, and as long as she lives, there will be no better place to be.

As the Uber made its way down Myrtle Ave., she visited the landmark, but her eyes were once again caught off guard by this nicely sealed envelope. It had no return address and when she finally opened it, it read: To my dearest granddaughter, I hope when you read this letter, you're happy and will have no regrets.

It's been 37 years, and I am up in age. Your grandfather died many years ago and I did not want to leave this earth without trying to explain some things to you. First of all, I would like to admit how much your grandfather and I regretted the choices we have made concerning you, your mother, and our only child. I'm not trying to make any excuses for us, but we came from an era where prejudices were allowed. Hopefully, having two parents from different nationalities did not place you in a line of fire. I'm so grateful that in today's time, people are not as cruel and those being judged are able to feel and speak up about any cruelty projected upon them. If it brings you any satisfaction, all those years without you in our lives were brutal and heart-wrenching. I know you're probably wondering why we never called or wrote. It was always something that we thought we would do eventually, and when we looked up, another day had passed, and the more skeptical we became. Our son meant everything to us and if you're a mother or will be one day, you would know the exact feeling. There is so much more I would love to say, but I would love to be able to see you. The choice is yours and if you never decide to make that happen, I just needed you to know how sorry and wrong we were. Growing up without your father had to be the saddest thing, but being a mother going through life without her child and being the reason why he doesn't exist was nothing you could ever imagine. So before ending this letter, not knowing where you are in life, we both may need this particular healing.

Love always, Patricia Jordan!

PS JUST LIKE THAT, HER LIFE HAD COME FULL CIRCLE IN AN INSTANT. NEVER DID SHE THINK HER FIRST TRAUMA IN LIFE WAS GOING TO BE THE LAST HEALING PART OF HER LIFE. THIS IS FOR ANYONE IN RECOVERY, NO MATTER WHAT THE ADDICTION IS. STAY TRYING, STAY FOCUSED, AND MOST DEFINITELY STAY PRAYED UP!

NEVER SAY GOODBYE, BUT SEE YOU LATER

ABOUT THE AUTHOR

Simone Bond

My name is originally Kim Simone McKie. When I got about 30 years old, I decided that I no longer felt like Kim but more like Simone. Therefore, Simone is the name I go by.

I attended Bay Ridge High. I dropped out of school two months prior to my graduation day. Later in life, I opted to take my GED. Schooling was very easy, but I allowed outside distractions to throw me off my path.

Once Simone emerged, so did many hidden talents. Once upon a time, I had my own cleaning and catering business. It was small-time, but it was all mine. I'm not one to brag, but I will admit I'm one badass!

I have three children, a loving husband, and one precious granddaughter. Out of all my passions, helping people and writing tugs at my heart. I am a loving and giving person, but unfortunately, sometimes, I am confronted by those that do not match my energy. That being said... Never say goodbye but see you later!

www.ingramcontent.com/pod-product-compliance
Lightning Source LLC
Chambersburg PA
CBHW051139120626
46547CB00012B/875